MW00414024

MIDLOTHIAN
FOLK
TALES

MIDLOTHIAN
FOLK TALES

LEA TAYLOR

ILLUSTRATED BY SYLVIA TROON

The History Press

For Angie Townsend (1967–2016),
much missed friend and storyteller.

And to my family and furry quadrupeds.

First published 2018

The History Press
The Mill, Brimscombe Port
Stroud, Gloucestershire, GL5 2QG
www.thehistorypress.co.uk

Text © Lea Taylor, 2018
Illustrations © Sylvia Troon, 2018

The right of Lea Taylor to be identified as the Author
of this work has been asserted in accordance with the
Copyright, Designs and Patents Act 1988.

All rights reserved. No part of this book may be reprinted
or reproduced or utilised in any form or by any electronic,
mechanical or other means, now known or hereafter invented,
including photocopying and recording, or in any information
storage or retrieval system, without the permission in writing
from the Publishers.

British Library Cataloguing in Publication Data.
A catalogue record for this book is available from the British Library.

ISBN 978 0 7509 8247 4

Typesetting and origination by The History Press
Printed and bound by CPI Group (UK) Ltd, Croydon, CR0 4YY

CONTENTS

FOREWORD

Lothian was one of the ancient kingdoms of Scotland, supposedly named after Loth who married the sister of King Arthur. It is now divided into three districts – East, West and Midlothian – each of which has its own distinctive landscape and character. Historically Edinburgh, the capital of Scotland, was part of Midlothian, but nowadays the rapidly growing city is a local authority area in its own right.

This has had two consequences. Midlothian, the hinterland of Edinburgh, has become hidden and often unnoticed. At the same time, people have forgotten that alongside its intellectual and artistic glories Edinburgh also has a local folklore. In this book, Lea Taylor, a Midlothian storyteller, sets out to correct both those perceptions by celebrating the stories of the older unified Midlothian, including Edinburgh.

To get beyond more recent stereotypes, Lea has gone out and about interviewing people, collecting local versions of well-known stories, while also uncovering snippets that have allowed her to resurrect some lost tales.

With a background in community education and a warm heart, Lea is ideally suited for this task. The result is genuinely fresh and carefully crafted to reflect the lives, loves and dreams of ordinary people who sustained themselves through Scotland's turbulent history, and the huge impacts of economic and social change. The stories in these pages give a direct flavour of the places, the people, the language, the humour, the hardship, and the phlegmatic determination to win through that has kept the area alive and distinctive through the centuries.

It is my hope that the many readers who will enjoy these tales will also get out and about in Midlothian. With places as diverse as medieval Newbattle and the National Mining Museum, Gorebridge village and the classical mansion at Arniston, remote Temple and busy Dalkeith, there is so much to see and visit. From country park to built environment, Midlothian has retained its own character and Lea Taylor's achievement in this book is to capture that, while whetting our curiosity to learn more. Long may she continue the invaluable work as a listener, sharer and teller in the great traditions of Scottish storytelling.

Donald Smith, 2017
Director, TRACS (Traditional Arts and Culture Scotland)

INTRODUCTION AND THANKS

In writing this book I have specifically sought out the oral tales told by local people where possible and then, in some instances, drawn upon other sources to check out their veracity. It was my intention to get a flavour of what the local inhabitants themselves felt were important stories, stories that are part and parcel of their landscape. In this way I was able to see the deeper connections folk had with their local environment and its rich history. Sometimes the information has come in the form of a passing reference, other times part of the tale or perhaps all of it, but a slightly differing version to one I may have picked up from another source. Some of the tales I have included have been part of my storytelling repertoire, while others are new and still finding their own unique expression. While I have recounted a few of the stories using my own voice, weaving fact, fiction and liberal sprinklings of creativity, there are others where I have deliberately tried to keep the local Scots voice intact. The book tends to follow a geographic theme, sourcing tales from different areas in and around Edinburgh and Midlothian.

Throughout the process I have met some wonderful people and experienced some interesting situations – stories in themselves.

This has been something of a journey – of exploration, finding out things about the area that I live in, learning new skills and

harking back to my undergraduate days at Edinburgh University, studying Scottish Ethnology. The oral tradition spoke to me just as powerfully then as it does now.

I came to storytelling through my grandfather 'Bick'. He had a way with words, whipping up anecdotal stories and peppering them with his Black Country dialect. The garden would echo with his voice and laughter as I sat captivated, drinking in all the imagery he created. In later years, working as a community worker, I saw storytelling in action and was smitten. I could see its power and potential for good within the communities I worked with. The power of story never ceases to amaze me – how it brings folk together, touches our hearts and minds and reminds us of what it is to be human.

I have so many people to thank for helping me with this book, particularly my family, for their patience – for teas uncooked, housework undone and family moments missed. A massive thank you to the extremely talented Sylvia Troon, storyteller, puppeteer and artist. Her illustrations for this book have literally brought the stories to life. Fortunately she had her memories of the area where she grew up to draw upon (Lasswade) and has kindly nudged and guided me along the way with some salient pieces of advice and encouragement.

Thanks also to Dalkeith Writers, particularly Stella Birrell and Catherine Simpson; Midlothian Libraries Archive Collection; also Claire Steele, who helped to start me off on this writing process. A huge debt of gratitude to all the people I interviewed and spoke with about the book; thank you for your time and patience. A big thank you to all the pupils of Lawfield Primary School, especially Primary 6b and their inspiring teacher, Avril Rodger, who have relished the local stories and given useful feedback. And finally, to all my friends and storytellers out there, past and present, for stories shared and stories yet to come – thank you.

ABOUT THE AUTHOR

LEA TAYLOR is passionate about storytelling's ability to inspire, inform, educate, enable and enlighten, and has extensive experience of delivering storytelling and training to family groups, schools, business, and community groups. Lea is no stranger to performance storytelling and has written and performed for stage and festival events across Scotland.

She lives in Midlothian with her husband, son and two dogs.

www.awaywithstories.co.uk

ABOUT THE ILLUSTRATOR

SYLVIA TROON studied Drawing and Painting at Edinburgh College of Art, and her career includes teaching, puppetry and oral storytelling. She illustrates her own stories, and has recently been providing illustrated castle and museum stories for Historic Environment Scotland.

www.sylviatroon.co.uk

1

AULD CRABBIT

Everyone in the town and surrounding areas knows of the crabbit auld wifey Mrs Fischer who lived in Bonnyrigg. Such was her reputation that her name was a by-word for bad-tempered. 'Crabbit as auld yin Fischer or you're as dour as Auld Crabbit,' they would say. She moaned and complained about everything, from the squeak on the neighbour's gate to the ringing of the church bells. She was never appeased and was thoroughly unpleasant to be around. Crabbit, crabbit, crabbit, like a broken record muttering under her breath, she would go tottering up the High Street laden down with her messages giving everyone the evil eye as she passed.

Apparently she was crabbit right from the outset. Even as a child she had perfected the whiny voice, turn-down smile and constant frown on her face, like she'd been sookin on a lemon some said. Others said worse, but I'm sure you get my drift.

Evidently there must have been at least some moment back in the day when she had been jolly and possibly kind, for she found herself a husband (poor unsuspecting soul) and settled in the older part of Bonnyrigg, where the big houses are, around the High Street. The marriage didn't last long. Her husband spent a lot of time working away, and as the years went by it became longer and longer until one day he didn't come back at all, which left Mrs Fischer alone at home to nurse her grievances and the ever-deepening bad temper.

The house was too big for Mrs Fischer. It was surrounded by a garden, laid to grass front and back, with a high stone wall at the boundary perimeter.

At the front of the house, situated next to the wall, was an old gnarled apple tree. To look at it you wouldn't have given it a second thought, but it yielded the best apples for miles around. Its reputation locally was legendary. Sweet and juicy yet crisp-to-bite apples they were. Many a child was seen to leap up while walking past and grab an apple. Indeed, small groups of them would go out on scrumping sorties.

Now Auld Crabbit would watch at the window, curtain twitching. When it came to harvest time we were all sure that she camped out by the window, lying in wait. It was her life's mission. Should anyone come down on her side of the road, a shadow would move behind the net curtains in her house, as if she were pressing her face close to the glass from behind the nets to get a better look, which was more than likely the case.

As soon as a child, or adult for that matter, made a move to take an apple, there she would be, railing and rattling at the window, screeching in her whiny voice, 'Get off my apples!' which mostly translated into a muffled shouting and banging at the window, the nets agitating wildly as if Punch and Judy had gone berserk behind the scenes.

If that wasn't enough to frighten off any potential offender, she would charge out of the front door and down the garden path in her baffies waving a great big stick and shouting, 'Be off, or I'll use it! A' ken yir faithers!' Generally, by the time she had reached the bottom of the garden path, the culprits would have beat a hasty retreat up the road, often collapsing in squeals of laughter and brandishing their booty in a taunting fashion.

As the years passed Auld Crabbit got more and more obsessed with the safety of her apples. Carefully she would gather her crop, taking them in to the deep recesses of her house, never to see the light of day again. We often wondered what she did with them. To our young minds it appeared she did nothing except guard them jealously, and probably crabbily too!

Late one lazy sunny autumn afternoon, when the boughs of the apple tree were laden with ripening fruit, a wide little old lady with hair the colour of a silver frost appeared walking up Auld Crabbit's road, and on *her* side too.

She slowed her pace as she neared the tree. She stopped and looked up into its branches. She closed her eyes and drew her head back as if breathing in the scent of the tree. Then, with a beaming smile, she opened Auld Crabbit's creaking wooden gate, walked up the garden path, and knocked at the door. Before long Auld Crabbit answered, having straightened her dress and checked her hair in the hall mirror beforehand. 'Yes?' she said, looking the little old lady up and down. 'What do you want?'

'Well, I hope you don't mind me being so presumptive but I wondered, might I have one of your apples?' The little old lady flashed one of her most dazzling smiles. 'They look and smell exactly like the kind of apples I used to eat with my father when I

was a little girl. It would be such a kindness if you allowed me to have one and I would be more than happy to pay you.'

Auld Crabbit was quite taken aback. Never in all her live-long days had anyone ever knocked at her door and asked permission to take one of her apples.

'Errrr,' and before she knew it, she said yes to the little old lady. 'Go ahead, help yourself.'

The little old lady was more than grateful – she was ecstatic! Auld Crabbit walked with her to the tree and watched as she picked a sweet, round red one. She gave it a rub over her coat sleeve so that it shone in the sunlight. Then she took a bite, closing her eyes as her teeth sank in.

'Mmmmmm, this tastes just as I remember it as a child. I really can't thank you enough. Now, I would like to offer you a kindness in exchange. You see, I am actually a fairy and I have the power to grant you a wish. So, tell me your heart's desire and I will see to it that it comes true.'

Staggered, Auld Crabbit was at a loss for words. She searched her mind for her dearest wish and then it came to her. A smile spread across her face. She hadn't smiled in years and it showed.

'My dearest wish,' she said in her cracked and grating voice, 'would be that anyone, apart from me, daring to take one of my apples gets stuck to the tree at the point where they tried to take it and they stay there until I say they can come down.'

'Oh. Really? Are you absolutely sure?'

'Positive,' said Auld Crabbit, nodding furiously.

'Very well then, so be it. Your wish is my command … oh, I do love saying that! Goodbye!' Then the little old lady simply faded away right before Auld Crabbit's eyes, leaving her staring into the space where the bitten apple hung suspended in mid-air.

Auld Crabbit went back indoors, made a cup of tea and a cheese and tomato sandwich, and waited with bated breath at the window. She didn't have to wait long and had only eaten half the sandwich when she spotted two figures at the end of the road. Stopping mid-munch she watched as the teenage boys walked jauntily towards the house. The hands-in-pockets, baggy jeans and hats-on-backwards type; yes, she knew them. Muttering under her breath she urged them to take an apple. 'That's it, yessssss, come closer …'

The boys stopped by the wall, peered over it then, after a backward glance, sprang up and grabbed an apple. The first lad, Mikey, swiped into the air but missed his target. The second, Kyle, made a direct connection. He let out a small whoop of elation and his face lit up with glee.

The excitement was short-lived though, turning to confusion, then shock and fear. For despite violent struggling he found he was stuck fast to the apple and the tree.

Mikey laughed at first, thinking it was a joke. However, Kyle's obvious struggles went a long way to explaining that something had gone badly wrong. In vain Mikey tried to pull his friend down. After half an hour he left, saying he would go and get help.

Auld Crabbit witnessed the spectacle with impish delight. She had a sneaking suspicion that she was going to really enjoy the fruits of her tree in more ways than she had ever imagined. She supped her tea and finished her sandwich, and decided she needed to get some messages.

Leaving the house, she cast a sideways glance at the boy hanging despondently from the tree and deliberately ignored his mewling pleas for help. Half an hour later Auld Crabbit returned with her messages.

A small crowd of young people had congregated around their friend. They stopped talking when she arrived; it gave her a sense of power and importance as she walked up the garden path. By the evening the young people had moved on, leaving Kyle to twist in the wind.

By 10 p.m. Auld Crabbit wanted him away and off her property. She told him she would release him on one condition: that he promise never to steal from her again and ensure that none of his friends did so either. Having obtained a pinkie promise, she freed him and that night slept peacefully for the first time in many years.

Word evidently spread around the neighbourhood. There was decidedly less footfall past the tree after Kyle's 'experience'. Auld Crabbit became more relaxed and even moved her chair away from the window. Many years passed and the tree and Auld Crabbit grew older.

Then, one evening just before Auld Crabbit's favourite soap was about to start on the telly, she heard the sound of the catch on the garden gate. Looking out of the window she watched as a strange tall character made its way up the garden path. Whether it was male or female she couldn't really tell, but she suspected it was a man by the size of its shoes.

It knocked a confident knock at the door. Rap, rap, rap. She opened it to a figure dressed in loose, black, long flowing clothes. Its face was partially covered with a hoodie and Auld Crabbit wasn't wearing her glasses so she couldn't precisely make out its features. In one of its bony hands it held a scythe.

'Good evening, Mrs Fischer.'

'That may as well be. What do you want?' She was irked because she could hear the strains of the theme tune of her favourite soap starting up.

'Do you know why I'm here?'

'No, and I'm not interested in your twenty questions either.'

'My name is Mr D'eath and I have come to inform you that your time has come. May I come in?'

'Do I have any choice?'

'No.'

Auld Crabbit opened the door and showed him into the front room.

'Do I have time to watch this programme? As a last request?'

'Oh very well,' said D'eath rather irritably as he slumped himself down on the sofa. He rummaged through his pockets and

fished out his mobile phone, then occupied himself with his text messages. For a fleeting moment Auld Crabbit wondered whether beneath the hood that shadowed his face he was wearing a hat, backwards.

After the programme had finished Auld Crabbit went into the kitchen and prepared herself some sandwiches in readiness for the journey. As she did so, she pondered over what she had achieved in her life. If only there were more time, she thought, as there were so many bad deeds she had left undone. D'eath had followed her, stopping to lean on the kitchen doorframe, and watched her. Nimbly she made herself a cheese and pickle sandwich and wrapped it carefully in silver foil. She hesitated, 'Oh, I need an apple. Would you be so kind as to go and fetch one for me from the tree in the garden? Take one for yourself too.' She attempted to fix a smile. Reluctantly D'eath went into the garden and reached up to a particularly delicious-looking sample. No sooner had his fingers touched the fruit when he found himself stuck fast, completely unable to get himself free. Auld Crabbit watched from her usual vantage point. A chuckle erupted from her mouth.

D'eath dangled from the apple tree for days. He had his uses: his flapping coat frightened off the birds.

Beyond the confines of Auld Crabbit's house things were going badly wrong. With D'eath otherwise engaged things in the real world had ground to a halt. Nothing was dying, funeral parlours were offering half-price deals, butchers were struggling, farmers were unable to move their stock, shops were running short of supplies.

Finally Auld Crabbit made the connection that the figure hanging from her apple tree might just have something to do with all the strange phenomena that were occurring elsewhere. Reluctantly she went to speak to D'eath.

'So, I've been thinking. I'll let you down on one condition, that you don't come for me until I say I'm ready.'

'This is most unusual, but given that I don't really have any choice …'

'I can't wait around all day,' said Auld Crabbit, making a point of looking at her watch.

'Oh very well. Agreed,' said D'eath rather resentfully. Auld Crabbit let D'eath down and watched as he stretched himself awkwardly before straightening up and heading off down the garden path. At the gate he paused to look back, raise his scythe and say, 'I'll be back.' For a moment Auld Crabbit was put in mind of the film *The Terminator*; he's not a patch on Arnie, she thought, and closed her front door.

The apple tree is still there at the foot of the garden. Nobody bothers to steal from it, though. Even now there are nets up at the window but whether or not Auld Crabbit is still there nobody knows for sure. Perhaps when the apples are ripe for picking we could try to steal one to find out?

This is a well-known Flemish tale, Old Misery, but can be found in various guises across Europe. I have added my own version of the tale – with a Scottish twist.

2

THE DOG'S
DISCOVERY

It was 1936, the weekend just before the long school summer holidays. A hot stifling day in July, the heat was oppressive. I remember lying in my bed, covers off, windows wide open, and still the room was airless. My father's snores filled the house like a slumbering bear.

On the day in question I'd gone round to Barry's; we were planning to meet the other lads to play down at Holyrood Park. Ron Milligan, one of our other cronies, would be back from his holidays – the family had gone camping down in the Borders; they go every year, same route. 'It's like the Holy Grail,' he would claim. 'We stop to visit all the relatives and come away with armfuls of goodies, especially boiled sweets.' With that in mind, it was vital that we got to Ron (and his sweets) before meeting the other lads – as they would scoff the lot before we got a look-in.

On that afternoon I brought Scruffy with me. He was our family dog. A wee terrier – with a terrier attitude and not always keen on other dogs, especially black ones like the one that lives next door to Mrs Resta. Without fail, they both go berserk when passing each other in the street. Hackles up and bared teeth. But aside from that wee detail, he was great as dogs go.

I can't quite remember now why I brought him with me. I think mum suggested it. He was a wilful dog and on that particular occasion had dug up dad's prize leeks. Dad went spare when he found out, chased him round the garden with his slipper in hand while we looked on from the kitchen window.

So Barry, me, and Scruffy the dog go and chap on Ron's door and we all head off to the Holyrood park stuffing Ron's sweets as we went. The others were already there. The usual game of kick the ba' begins. We all run about in earnest trying to gain possession, then Scruffy starts darting in and out. He makes great sport of racing after the ball and tackling, despite our fierce boots, so much so we all end up yelling at him in varying tones of exasperation, 'Scruffy, leave!'. Eventually he gave up and found something else to occupy him.

We got so caught up in the game that I didn't notice that the dog had completely disappeared. The score was evens, two goals apiece. Then, as the afternoon progressed, each of the lads peeled away, one by one, to go home for their tea. All that remained were Barry, Ron and me. It was then that we realised that Scruffy was away. Missing.

We set up a search party round the park, running up and down the brae calling his name and whistling. Stopping folk to ask if they'd seen a wee black and white terrier with two brown splodges around the eyes – like an unusual pair of glasses – that answered to the name of Scruffy. No one had seen him; my heart was beginning to sink. How could I return home without him?

I stood still, desperate, my heart pounding, then I heard it, clear above the sounds of the city: a high-pitched yip, followed by excited barking. There followed a long moment of quiet, then another yip. We all began to run at the same time towards where the sound came from, stopping at the top. We stopped at the top of the hill just below Arthur's Seat.

At first we couldn't see anything – it was all shadow on that particular side of the hill and the late afternoon sun was in our eyes. Something moved down in the far corner. A flash of a wagging white tail, then the yip came again.

As we got closer I could see Scruffy's head thrust down a hole and busy digging, his front paws working furiously against the soil, mud flying everywhere. He had found something. A rabbit perhaps? By the time we reached him, there was something in his jaws; it looked a bit like a wee ragdoll. As I approached him he gave a playful growl and set his front paws flat in that 'come play with me manner' that he has. When I reached to grab his new-found prize, which was firmly grasped between his jaws, he darted away. It took several unsuccessful attempts to catch him.

Finally I got his attention with what was left of Ron's sweets, the last remaining bullseye. He dropped the doll at the place near to where he had been digging.

We didn't really notice it at first. Three pieces of slate, partially covering a shallow cave in one of the rocks. It was only then that I noticed a wee wooden box, a curious box about four inches long, shaped like a small coffin with its lid prised off. It had evidently been there for quite a while as the wood was delicate and felt damp and slimy. On picking it up I spied the corner of another similar box sticking out of the mud. I scraped the earth back to reveal another, and another. Ron and Barry knelt down to help and eventually we managed to excavate the sum total of seventeen of these little coffins.

Recklessly we prised off the lids from a few of them and found that each contained a strange ragdoll, dressed in clothes according to their gender. It felt a bit macabre as we couldn't figure out why they would be there. Then Ron started to lark about, pretending

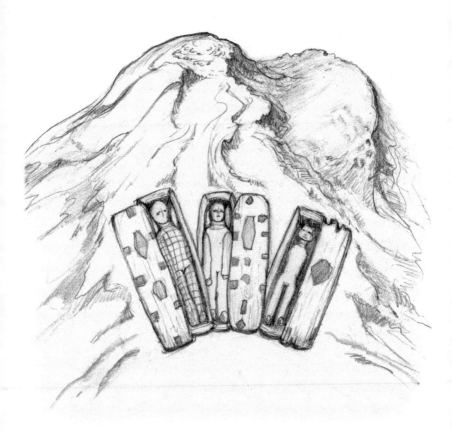

that one of the dolls had suddenly come alive, complete with ghoulish gait and voice. We each seized a doll and ran about in the gloaming, chasing each other with Scruffy barking and nipping at our heels. After a while we tired of the game and decided to make for home. As an afterthought I suggested we bring some of the coffins and their contents home with us; we could take them into school the next day. The rest we stuffed back into the cave and covered the entrance with the slates.

The following morning I put my find, a small coffin containing a male doll, into my desk. Every time Mr Sinclair turned his back to us to write on the board I would quickly bring it out and make it dance on the back of Ron's head. He was seated at the desk in front of me. Soon the whole class was laughing at my antics; Mr Sinclair was not impressed with the interruptions. Finally he whirled round, catching me red-handed larking about.

He ordered me to bring it to the front of the class. I remember so clearly the sense of shame as I walked slowly up the class to his desk, all eyes on me and all of my classmates thinking, 'He's going to get the tawse now'. The bell went at the moment I reached the desk, and my classmates filed out in quick fashion. I stood quaking beneath Mr Sinclair's death stare.

'What is it?' he demanded, holding his hand out. I placed the doll and coffin in his outstretched palm.

'I don't really know, Sir. We found it at Holyrood Park, near Arthur's Seat. There were loads of them, well, seventeen altogether.'

The anger was gone from his face and had been replaced with avid curiosity. 'Intriguing. Seventeen of them you say? Were they all dressed like this?'

'Yes, Sir, but some were women and some were men.'

'Lawson, would you mind if I held on to this to see if I could find out more information about it?' I nodded. 'You see, I'm an amateur archaeologist and a member of the local archaeological society – this looks like a very interesting find indeed. I take it you could show me the spot where you found them again?'

'Yes, Sir,' I nodded. 'But it's my dog, Scruffy, that should get the credit. He was the one that found them.'

I left the classroom more relieved at not having received the tawse than eager to know about the origins of the coffins and their contents.

Despite Mr Sinclair's extensive enquiries there was nothing to explain the existence of the coffins. The only information he was able to give me was that the oldest coffin had been put in the cave many years before but at least one of them, it was felt, had been quite a recent addition.

Eight of the coffins are now on display in the National Museum of Scotland, an enigma in their own right. Some folk are inclined to think that coffins and their contents represent the bodies of the victims of Burke and Hare. Part of the culture and belief at that particular time was that if a body wasn't whole and complete on the day of judgement, how could God recognise or accept the individual? Others believe that they represent good luck charms for seafarers, while some are convinced that these wee coffins and their contents belong to the wee folk. I'll leave it up to you to decide.

This is a fairly well-known and popular story among Edinburgh's local storytellers, but I first heard tell of this tale from the wonderful David Campbell.

3

AN UNLIKELY AUCTION

This is one of my favourite stories, reported in a broadside some three hundred years ago. The event lends itself to the rich texture of Edinburgh life in an age gone by – assuming that activities such as this don't happen over the Internet, or do they?

If I stand in the middle of Edinburgh's Grassmarket, close my eyes and take in the hustle and bustle of the place, I can almost see the event unfold.

It wasn't as if he was being unreasonable. Every other man he knew had a wife he could come home to, be greeted with a civil smile, a plate of warm food on the table, and the hearth and house in neat and clean order. There was no excuse; there were no children to attend to, yet.

Twice that week he had come home to find his wife, Mary, passed out on the floor. Empty bottles at her side and the house in disarray. As Thomas Guisgan stood over her he nudged her with the toe of his boot. She murmured, opened her bleary eyes and squinted at him before turning her face away, muttering her irritation. Words stumbled out of her mouth as if colliding into each other. He could make no sense of what she was saying but smelt the familiar stench of stale porter. Bile rose in the back of his throat; anger pure and simple made him gag and gasp. It was one

thing to have a slovenly wife, but to have a wife a slave to the porter
was too hard to accept. His honour and reputation were at stake
and she was beyond his help or tolerance. He resolved to find a
solution, one that would accommodate both of their needs.

Leaving her lying on the cold stone floor, her dark hair fanned
out around her, he stepped back out into the night. The crisp air
helped to clear his mind as he wandered through the fog, passing
shadowy figures. He made his way along the Grassmarket, then up
Lady Lawson Street to the auctioneer's office. There was a flicker of
light from within. Someone was still there.

His fists beat loudly on the door, perhaps a little overzealous, but better to take it out on the door than elsewhere. The startled clerk put his pen down and shuffled to answer it. Opening cautiously he peered out, 'Sir, I was just about to …'

'I'll not take much of your time.' Guisgan brushed past, bringing the cold night air in with him.

After the formalities had been exchanged, the elderly clerk sat back in his chair and let out a long sigh and made a bridge with his stubby ink-stained fingers. 'Your request is most unusual, but I am sure it can be accommodated. We will, of course, levy our usual fees for our services and rest assured we will attend to all the necessary notices for a …' he hesitates for a second and a smile passes his lips, 'meagre sum.' Guisgan reached into his pocket, pulled out a small leather purse and placed the coins on the counter.

'Until Thursday then, Sir.'

'Until Thursday.'

It was an exceptionally large crowd that gathered in the Grassmarket that day. There was an air of expectant anticipation. Several stallholders had pitched their stands closer to the auction house, as if they knew today would be a day for swift trade, and they were not disappointed. By 6 p.m. some two thousand people had gathered and more were still coming.

Guisgan arrived, feeding the spectacle by leading his wife with a makeshift straw rope tied around her waist and a notice pinned to her bosom with the words 'to be sold by public auction'. The crowd fell silent and shifted uneasily as Thomas Guisgan and his forlorn wife stepped through.

It started off fairly civilly. Mary McIntosh, Guisgan's wife, was made to climb up onto a wee platform for her to be seen above the crowd. It quietened momentarily as a sea of expectant faces took in the scene. Mary was fair of face, her dark hair had been braided and tied up to show her high cheekbones and bright, engaging blue eyes. Her face flushed as she cast her gaze down, making her appear vulnerable and innocent. When the church clock rang out the last of its chimes for six o'clock, the auctioneer took to his lectern, his white hair standing out against the grey evening light. Gavel in hand he struck the desk to gain everybody's attention. He wrestled to be heard above the clamouring crowd; the babbling had risen from hushed tones to a swell of derisive shouts as the mass surged and swayed. He banged his gavel down again and again but the crowd was beginning to jostle and collide as more folk arrived to witness the event.

The bidding started. The first bid came as a shout from the crowd, and a Highland drover stepped through. He looked rough and unshaven, his broad shoulders swathed in a heavy plaid. He stood before the auctioneer, pulled out his purse and said, 'She be a guid like lassie, I will gie ten and twenty shillings for her.' The crowd gave a rousing cheer but his bid was bettered by a stout tinker who bolted up the front, bowling people out of his way. His rich voice rose above the noise. 'She should never go to the Highlands before offering a sixpence.' The crowd laughed indulgently.

Next up came a bid from a Killarney pig jobber, with a mouth as wide as a turnpike gate. His face was red and his eyes looked in opposite directions, and had it not been for the crowd pressing and clamouring against each other it's highly possibly the pig jobber would have fallen flat on his face.

Half-drunk, he offered a further two shillings more given that she was a 'pratty' (or mischievous) woman. By this point the mood of the crowd was beginning to change. Then a brogue maker, having just emerged from an alehouse as drunk as fifty cats in a wallet, stepped forward and hit the Killarney man full on the nose, knocking him out for a good ten minutes.

Standing at close quarters and witnessing the whole thing, Mary McIntosh laughed heartily and the crowd joined in, giving long and incessant cheers. But the scene deteriorated rapidly as bare-knuckle fighting broke out – much of it carried out by women armed with stones. Then, the drunken brogue maker walked up to the auctioneer and knocked him and the lectern down; his mug of claret flowed freely all over the floor.

By this time the neighbourhood women had gathered, all seven hundred of them, and they had a look of militant intent. Initially they stood on the perimeter of the crowd armed with stones, some of which were loaded into stockings or handkerchiefs while others threw them freely. Then they made a general charge through the mob, knocking down everyone that came their way until they finally reached the auctioneer. He cowered behind the lectern, pleading loudly that he should be left alone. The furious women set upon him, scratched and tore at his face in a terrifying manner, screeching at the top of their voices, utterly vexed by the insult the fair sex had received.

The crowd looked on aghast. One women, the wife of a sweep, later described as a true herione, suddenly spied Thomas Guisgan and let vent her anger by pelting him with stones; after all, he was the cause of all the commotion. Above the din her voice could be heard calling him all kinds of vile names, but mostly the words 'contaminated villain' carried across the Grassmarket. Guisgan, who was evidently not known for his gentlemanly airs, retaliated against the assault and punched the wifey smartly between the eyes, leaving them like two October cabbages.

A general battle ensued and, had it not been for police intervention, lives surely would have been lost. After a while the worst of the rammy was quelled and the crowd stood waiting for the auction to recommence.

Once again Mary was brought up before the crowd. At this point an elderly seaman, Jack Tar, stepped forward and indicated his interest while using the words 'well rigged' to describe her. The auctioneer, having suitably recovered from his earlier encounter, took a note of his offer for half a crown, which was more than the previous bidder. But Jack Tar was soon disappointed and his offer

topped by a farmer, said to be a widower, who pledged two pounds and five shillings. The sale was agreed and the gavel hit the lectern to confirm the sale.

The farmer led Mary McIntosh away through the crowd to where his horse stood patiently waiting. There he mounted his horse and took Mary up behind him. They rode away midst the cheers of the populace. There never was another auction of this ilk held again.

For anyone wishing to see the actual broadside it can be found in the National Library of Scotland: Lauriston Catalogue L.C. 1268(092): Sale of Wife.

4

THE NEWHAVEN WILLOW

Oh weel may the boatie row,
And muckle may she speed,
Weel may the boatie row,
That wins oor bairnies' breid,
The Boatie Rows.

John Ewen (1741–1821)

It was just the other day that I happened to be in the area of
Newhaven. I wondered at the change from the sleepy hamlet and
harbour it had once been back in the 1700s, home to a tight-knit
and thriving fishing community, the majority of whom were
involved with seafaring activities, from fishing to whaling and
landing oysters. As I stood looking at the shoreline it brought to
mind an old tale related to this very area. I was left wondering
where the giant willow associated with the tale might have been
sighted, for it, and any evidence of it, is sadly long gone now.

According to the story there was once a fisherman's wife called
Betsy. She was a Bow-Tow, a born and bred Newhavener, and
proud of it. Being young and newlywed with a wee bairn, she had
gone to the shoreline to look out for her husband's boat and greet
him on his return. In her arms she carried their bairn all snuggled
up in a new wicker cradle. It smelled of freshly cut withies and

creaked just as I imagine the tree boughs would, straining in the wind. After standing and waiting for some time, Betsy caught sight of her husband's boat far off on the horizon, its small white sail billowing in the wind.

As she stood there watching the boat approaching, ploughing its way up the Forth, anticipating the warmth of her husband's embrace, the skies suddenly turned grey-white. A fierce north wind whipped up out of nowhere, frothing the waves into foaming fury and with its giant hands tossed the whirling water to the skies. Such was its force that the poor lass could barely stand, let alone hang on to her child in its cradle. The wind lashed itself around her, lifting her skirt and petticoats to reveal white worsted stockings. She staggered back up the shoreline and sought shelter at the mouth of one of the closes.

Generally from that vantage point the seashore and any boats coming in to harbour could be seen, but Betsy could see nothing – nothing but a white wall of flurrying snow. The wind howled and raged for what seemed like an eternity and so the young fisherman's wife hunkered down, pulled the baby and cradle close, and sang a soft lullaby to her sleepy child.

'Oh weel may the boatie row, and muckle may she speed ...'

Finally the ferocity of the blizzard abated: the snow still drifted slowly down but visibility had returned.

Betsy stood up, dusted herself down and looked seaward. Although her fingers and toes were numb she picked up her bairn and made her way down the beach to the shoreline. The sand and stones carried a light dusting of snow that dissolved almost as soon as it landed. She searched the horizon for her husband's boat. It took a minute or two before she was able to spot it bobbing up and down on the waves. 'There, there it is.' She took a sharp intake of breath and went up on tiptoes, straining to see.

'Look, Nellie, look. It's your Daddy come home.'

A smile settled momentarily on her lips and then she froze. Her whole body signalled distress. What she saw was a hull listing awkwardly, like a fish without a swim bladder. It was obvious that the boat was merely drifting, its mast and sail torn down by the force of the wind. Nowhere, on boat or water, could she see any evidence of her husband. For a good few minutes she stood there, desperately scanning the skyline. Big tears welled up and trickled down her cold pink cheeks, her heart felt as if it would surely burst. Clutching on to her baby's cradle she stood and sobbed, wailing at the sea.

Perhaps it was the cold, perhaps it was the lack of food, perhaps it was the shock at realising she was a widow, or more than likely the mix of all three that did it. Betsy's frail young body crumpled

on that shoreline with the sea's fingers reaching up the beach and retreating back into the Forth waters. As she and her child lay on the frozen sand, snow eddied and covered them softly as the cold steadily claimed them.

It did not take long for the villagers of Newhaven to find their frozen bodies on the seashore. Reverently they took them home and buried them in the local graveyard.

The cradle had been caught on the tide, carried a little and eventually thrown back on the beach. It had been left there deliberately for nature to follow her will, to rot or let the tide take it, for superstition and a sense of respect for a lost community member was strong.

The baby's cradle was new, had only been made some months beforehand. The woven rods used to make it were mere saplings, ripe and pliable. The following spring a small shoot appeared. Over the years it grew steadily into a beautiful, majestic willow tree; tall and strong with a thick wide girth, its fronds dancing and rustling in the wind.

Soon it became a place of play; children climbed its branches, young lovers used it as a meeting point. Fishermen looked out for it, a familiar landmark, a sign to say they were nearly home.

As time passed the tree developed its very own folk tale. An old spaewife, known in the community to have the gift of prophesy, foretold that the tree would become a landmark for the harbour and the seafaring community. She also said that 'as long as the tree flourished, the village would prosper'. It would only fall when 'the fishing trade left Newhaven' or when 'great decked boats fit to face the German ocean, even in winter, set sail from the harbour'.

She was not far from the mark with her prediction. The nineteenth century heralded the coming of the trawling boats; their presence adversely affected the profits and fortunes of traditional fishing.

Then one stormy night a huge branch tumbled from the tree. The Newhaven community was in an uproar. The fallen branch was perceived as a bad omen. Up in arms, the fishermen took things further and made threats against the trawler men. At this juncture a Free Church Minister of Newhaven, a certain Reverend James Fairbairn, intervened and reminded the people of a particular clause in the prophecy: 'When great decked boats ... set sail from the harbour.'

The Minister had foresight, he saw that the community boats were out of date for modern requirements. He encouraged them to build a new fishing fleet. One fit for purpose by proposing a reconstruction that entailed boats with decks, bunks and other compartments.

This was all made possible because Fairbairn himself lent the fishermen the money to carry this out. Over time, thirty-eight large new boats were built for the grand sum of £250 each.

The much awaited day of celebrations came. Sailing from the harbour to much fanfare and honking of horns, Reverend James

Fairbairn led the fleet of decked crafted in a boat named in his honour.

Only when the last of the small boats were hauled to shore permanently did the enormous willow tree finally fall, its mission fulfilled, marking the end of an era.

The Reverend was able to see out the new beginnings of the fishing fleet and the changes it brought to the community, meeting his maker in 1879.

A picture of Reverend James Fairbairn currently exists within the National Media Museum dated *c.* 1845 and entitled 'Fairbairn reading to the Fishwives'. I wonder if he ever read the story of Betsy and the willow tree's early beginnings?

A big thank you to Dode Muir, musician and artist, for pointing me in the direction of this little-known but intriguing story.

5

EDINBURGH ROYAL OBSERVATORY'S ENIGMA

A man in his mid-thirties sits at the wheel of a large motorcar. He cuts the engine and strikes a match, and it flares in the darkness before lighting the cigarette. Quietly, two figures slip away from the vehicle and run, keeping close to the bushes along the road. After a while they disappear into blackness. He waits with bated breath, flicking ash from his sleeve and keeping lookout. The clock on the dashboard reads 12.45 a.m.

A flash of light is followed by a loud bang which ricochets around the hillside. Then he hears the quickened footsteps, moving at speed as they get nearer to the motorcar. From his rear-view mirror he can see one of the figures is hurt, hunched over and limping heavily, aided by the other. The rear door wrenches open and two bodies fall inside, breathing heavily.

'Quick, Teddy, start the car. Millicent's been hurt.'

Deftly, Teddy leaps from his seat and begins cranking the car. It takes two attempts before it springs into life. The party find themselves hurtling down Observatory Road. In the back seat two women sit pale and wan.

'Millicent, keep still dear while I put a tourniquet on your wrist. Does it hurt very much? You're bleeding badly.'

Agnes leans forward in an attempt to simultaneously support her injured friend and tear a strip of material from her petticoat. With some effort she manages it.

'What on earth happened back there?' shouts Teddy, half turning to look behind.

'Just keep your eye on the road and head straight for the safe house as fast as you can, please,' says Agnes. 'She's losing far too much blood.'

The big yellow motorcar rumbles its way through the dark streets until eventually it turns down a long driveway; tyres crunch on gravel as it draws to a stop. Agnes looks out the window at a large imposing Victorian house wrapped in darkness, curtains drawn shut against the world beyond.

She jumps out of the car, runs up the path to the front door and bangs impatiently. Somewhere deep inside a light goes on and movement can be heard. It seems to take an age before anyone comes. In loud whispers Agnes directs Teddy in removing the now unconscious Millicent from the car. Carefully he carries her limp body into the house.

Tearfully Agnes tells her hostess, Gwen, what has happened. 'It's all my fault. I should never have allowed her to do it. We had it all planned; *I* was going to light the fuse and set the thing off. After all, I was the one that took the instructions on how to do it. It was terribly windy and the matches kept going out – that and the fact that it was pitch black up there. Milly got rather impatient and snatched the matches from me. She managed to light the fuse, but instead of lighting the end, she dithered and lit it half way. It took; that's when I started to run, but then it fizzled out. I looked back and saw her trying to light the fuse again. I wanted to shout but didn't dare. Next thing I knew there was an almighty bang and Milly was thrown backwards from the force. She lay on the floor, not moving.' Agnes begins to sob, fumbling in her pocket for a handkerchief. She blows her nose and continues. 'I ran, heaved her up and had to drag her back to the car.'

With an air of calm Gwen checks Millicent over. Her small pale hands with short scrubbed fingernails are meticulous yet gentle. She turns to face Agnes; the frown on her forehead speaks volumes.

'It looks like her hand has taken the brunt of the blast. It's in a bad way but I think we can save it. She'll need a lot of rest and her wound will need dressing daily if you want to spare it from infection. You know you won't be able to stay here indefinitely, don't you? Three days and we'll have to find you another safe house.'

Agnes nods, taking in all the implications. Across the room Teddy is sitting on a chair, shoulders hunched and staring at the floor, clenching his teeth. 'Teddy, do you think you can cover for Millicent? Explain to the Heriots that she was called away on urgent family business.' He inclines his head but doesn't look at her, makes to start for the front door then stops mid-stride and turns. 'I need an explanation. You could have died back there – both of you. I would never have gone along with this confounded business had I known that this is what you were up to. I'm all for Votes for Women, but not acts of terrorism.' His face was set. 'I thought you were going to put a brick through a window; that that was what you were carrying in your bag.'

For a split second Agnes faltered. 'Oh no, the bag!' She looks about her person, gripped in panic. 'I've left it back there.'

Teddy stiffens. 'Lord, is there anything incriminating in it?'

Agnes pauses. 'I, I don't know. Wait. I have to think … No, I don't think so.'

'Are you sure?' says Teddy in earnest.

Agnes searches her mind's eye once again and after a moment her frown turns into a mischievous smile. 'No. Definitely not.' She is now thinking of the bag's contents: a few currant biscuits wrapped in paper, a couple of safety pins and a carefully folded scrap of paper upon which she had written, in her best handwriting, 'How beggarly appears argument before defiant deed – VOTES FOR WOMEN'. The intention was to leave the note at the scene of the crime. She thinks back to when she and Millicent wrote it. They had been to a 'meeting', the speaker had inspired them. Emboldened by Emmeline Pankhurst's edict, 'It is our duty to break the law in order to call attention to the reasons why we do it. Deeds not words,' they had both put their names forward to take part. They were scrupulous in their planning; coached and encouraged by other more qualified members of the Women's Social and Political Union (WSPU), their education began in earnest. When they got to the point of writing the note they laughed at their brazenness. She remembered that moment when she saw her own reflection in Millicent's smiling eyes and for a split second hardly recognised herself.

She looks down at her friend, lying quiet and still, her dark hair in contrast to the white pillow, flecks of reddy-brown blood on her starched collar. Millicent stirs and her eyes flicker open. In a weak voice she asks, 'Is it done? Did we succeed?'

Agnes leans down and tries to pacify her. 'Shhhh now, Milly, don't try to move. We're at the safe house. You've hurt your hand but it'll mend. You need to rest, but yes, mission accomplished.'

Later, while taking hot cocoa in the drawing room, Gwen advises Agnes that it's not safe to venture outside. Word has been sent to the WSPU that a new safe house is urgently required. Agnes' hands shake as she holds the hot mug. Her heart pounds deep in her chest, her breath shallow. She listens, hears her hostess's words, but they do not land. She is still marvelling at the gallusness of her actions – the act of merely slamming a door prior to this would have sent her into paroxysms of fear and trembling. She was even frightened of her own shadow. But meeting Millicent and attending the WSPU meetings had brought about a change in her.

No longer is she meek and pliant, a mere chattel. No! She is her own woman and prepared to fight for that right and for her sisters in arms. She lifts her chin in defiance.

This is a true story which I have taken the liberty of fictionalising. The Edinburgh Royal Observatory was indeed attacked by suffragettes. The perpetrator was never caught following the blast that shattered windows, splintered floors and cracked stone on the observatory's tower on 21 May 1913. The bomb, a jar with gunpowder, exploded at 1 a.m. when nobody was inside to be injured. A ladies' handbag containing currant biscuits, safety pins and a note were found at the scene, along with a pool of blood. Written in ink on a scrap of paper was the phrase: 'How beggarly appears argument before defiant deed. Votes for women.'

I first came across this story while on holiday with my husband, who happens to be an astronomer working at Edinburgh Royal Observatory. It was a small give-away sentence, delivered in such a manner that I accidentally spat my drink out all over him. Thanks also to Pippa Goldschmidt's article (ROE website) on the event.

6

THE GILMERTON
STOORWORM

The following story is about Gilmerton, an area in Edinburgh I once had the privilege to work in. At the time some of the members of the local community were working hard to develop and restore Gilmerton Cove and open it to the general public.

Gilmerton Cove is an intriguing series of underground passageways and chambers hand-carved from sandstone located beneath the streets of Gilmerton, an ex-mining village, now a suburb of Edinburgh.

There are many theories about the origins of the Cove and its purpose. It is known that it was the eighteenth-century residence of local blacksmith, George Paterson. The parish records show that he was reprimanded for allowing alcohol to be consumed within the Cove on the Sabbath. It is not known whether Paterson was responsible for carving the Cove.

Popular theories are that it was used as a drinking den for local gentry, a Covenanters' refuge, and a smugglers' lair. Extensive archaeological and historical research has failed to resolve the mystery. This is my take on the tale of Gilmerton Cove.

A long time ago in a little backwater to the south-east of Edinburgh, there lived a blacksmith. He was the seventh son of a seventh son, a blacksmith like his father and his father before him, and the only one of his siblings to follow in his father's footsteps and take up the trade. When his father died, he inherited the forge, the cottage and all its contents. He was a young man, newly wed and full of optimism. Things went well for a number of years, the business picked up and his wife gave birth to a beautiful baby girl.

The day came when hard times were brought to his door. His wife fell ill with a fever and died. He found himself a widower with a grief-stricken teenage daughter. At the same time business had dropped, passing trade had slowed – people were less inclined to travel. There were reports that a strange and dangerous creature was at large in the city. A creature that had never been seen by anyone left alive to bear witness. Rumours were rife. The blacksmith was struggling. He retreated into his forge, worked the great bellows on the fire and spent his days manipulating molten iron with hammer and anvil. All that could be heard was the steady clang of hammer on metal.

In the house his daughter continued her mother's chores. She was a beauty with fair skin and sparkling blue eyes framed by silken tresses that shone gold, yellow and red in the sun. Yet despite her beauty she had few friends. She was lonely and longed for her mother.

One day she sat down at the kitchen table and wept. Her tears fell in puddles and ran in rivulets along the floor to a small hole at the far end of the kitchen. After a while a muffled voice cried out, 'Please stop crying. Your salty tears are hurting me.' The girl looked around her but could not find the owner of the voice. Had she had imagined it? A single tear ran down her face and landed on the floor. She watched it trickle to the corner of the kitchen like the rest of the tears, where it disappeared down a hole. 'Ouch!' cried the voice. Startled, the girl jumped up and tried to peer down the hole. It was black and she could see nothing. She sat back a moment and then spied a small inconspicuous trapdoor half-hidden beneath the sideboard. She tugged and heaved at the sideboard so that she could get to the trapdoor. So curious was she that she opened it and then, taking a lit candle with her, descended the dusty wooden steps.

There, far below the kitchen, was a deep cavernous room hewn out of the sandstone rock. In its centre stood a long table surrounded by seats made in a similar fashion to that of the room.

Something moved in the shadows and two small green lights shone back at her. She held up her candle. There in the corner lay a hideous-looking creature – a great big oversized worm blinking its pink-rimmed eyes against the light. On its blubbery white body were red blotches, some of which had blistered and were weeping.

'I'm allergic to salt,' it sniffed.

'Did my tears do that?' She pointed to the offending welts. The worm nodded.

'I'm so sorry,' said the girl. 'Would you like a salve?'

The worm merely blinked and tried to turn around a little more to face her fully. Its great folds of flesh rippled as it moved and a noise, not unlike a fart, was emitted. An awkward moment passed between them. The girl made to turn and go. 'Please don't leave,' said the worm. 'Stay and keep me company a while – it's the least you could do.'

So the girl stayed, taking a seat at the table, and they chatted about this and that. He served her tea and cakes, the most delicious she had ever tasted. They played chess while the worm smoked a hookah pipe. As the smoke curled around the cavern the girl felt quite dreamy and intoxicated. So much so that she lost all sense of time and, before long, fell into a deep sleep.

The blacksmith returned home to find his daughter gone without a trace. There was nothing to indicate where she might be. The only odd thing was a slight trail of slime across the kitchen tiles. Three days and nights passed and there was still no sign of his daughter. He was fraught with worry. In the city there had been reports of a hideous creature taking people unawares. Most of the bodies turned up in the mines and there were plenty of mines to be found around the city.

That evening an old traveller appeared at the smithy. His horse had thrown a shoe and needed to be reshod. The blacksmith should have shut his doors for the night but he took pity on the traveller. As the blacksmith waited for the furnace to heat up, the traveller studied him. 'I have the gift of prophecy,' he said. 'Would you like me to share with you what I see?' Normally the blacksmith would shun such an offer but he was desperate.

'What you seek is beneath you. You will find your daughter but will need the faery folk's assistance. They will help for a price. Go and forge a silver sword fit for their king.'

'But how will I find the faery folk?' asked the blacksmith.

'Tomorrow night, at midnight, you must go to Ellen's Glen and take the sword. There you will see a mound that has neither heather nor gorse on it and when the moon is neither dark nor light, stamp three times upon it and the faery folk will open their world to you. You will need to be strong and brave of heart for I cannot guarantee that you will be successful in your quest as no one has ever been to that world and returned to tell their tale.'

The blacksmith worked all through the night. He crafted the finest sword ever seen and etched upon it the most exquisite elaborate patterns. The next night, just before midnight, he set off for Ellen's Glen. The harvest moon was full and bright, yet he worried he might not find the faery knoll. With a heavy heart he searched, unsure where to look, but love and determination drove him on. Finally he found the knoll, way down in the glen. It was covered with neither heather nor gorse. Embedded in it were little white stones that shimmered in the light. He drew himself up tall, took a deep breath and waited until the moon was shadowed by a cloud so that it was neither dark nor light. Then the blacksmith stamped three times.

From beneath the knoll came a reedy voice, 'Who's there?'

'A mortal blacksmith.'

'What do you want?'

'I want to enter your kingdom.'

There was a cackle. 'A mortal, enter our world? If you do you take your life in your hands, but enter, by all means – and say goodbye to all you have known and loved.'

With the blink of an eye, the blacksmith found himself standing inside the faery knoll. He could not see an obvious way in or out and got the sensation of a dreich biting cold that made its way to the marrow of his bones.

About him shadows darted back and forth. Fingers of unseen bodies nipped at him, pulled his hair and poked him from all directions. Wings fluttered in the air and the hint of whispers played around him. The blacksmith stepped boldly forward; he stumbled and slipped in the dark against the rocks, moss and leaves. He forced his way past vines and great roots dangling from the earth. Mud and stones fell onto his face and hair as he pushed.

Eventually he emerged into a cavernous room filled with faeries. Ephemeral wings flitted and buzzed past him; he felt the air move as they went.

The room quietened to a hush. The king of the faeries was paraded in on his mossy throne to a trumpet fanfare. Everyone bowed. He wore a crown of golden leaves and about his shoulders he carried a silken cloak stitched with strands of spiders' web. He smiled but his eyes were cold.

The faery king spoke. 'And what brings you to our world, mortal?'

'I am a blacksmith of high repute and have come to seek your help.'

'Why should we help you?' The king stroked his silken cloak and examined its bejewelled clasp.

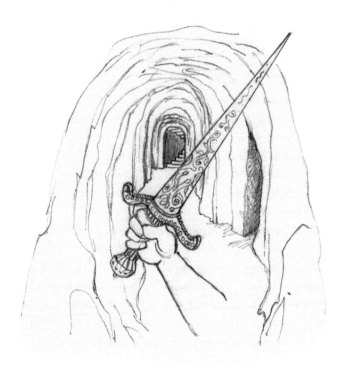

'Someone has taken my daughter. I was told on good authority that you were my only hope. I have made you a special gift in exchange.' As he held the sword out to the king everyone gasped. The king took it in trembling hands. 'A sword fit to slay the beast,' he whispered. 'You may leave. We have work to be done! We may call upon your skills another time.'

The king arose and a flurry of winged faeries followed in his wake. Before the blacksmith had time to ask a question he found himself standing above the faery mound in Ellen's Glen. The moon slid from behind its cloud to shine a pathway home.

The blacksmith's daughter was awoken by a strange screeching sound. She tried to move but found that her hands and feet were bound. There was barely any light but she could just about make out the frame of a door around which light crept in. Beyond, a great struggle was taking place. Eventually all went quiet; she lay in the semi dark trying not to despair, but so many thoughts were racing through her mind. Finally footsteps approached, the door opened and a handsome young man stepped in. Swiftly and gently he untied her hands and feet and spoke to her in reassuring tones. She knew that voice and looked at him quizzically. 'Who are you …and where am I?'

'I am Loth, son of Loth. I have been trapped down here for many years in the guise of a great worm, made to do the bidding of the evil stoorworm who captured me and put me under a spell.'

'But where am I exactly and why was I bound?' asked the daughter, confused and distressed.

'You are in a cavern beneath your cottage and father's forge. It is part of a network of tunnels that reach far across the city. They have been used by miners and the faery folk for many years, but more recently put to no good purposes by the stoorworm – a great and frightful beast who came from afar. He took refuge here from a storm and decided he liked the place so much he wanted to stay.

'I was the one who bound you – to keep you safe and out of the stoorworm's sight. But you have nothing more to fear; the faery folk have put paid to him now, thanks to your father. The enchantment could only be broken by a silver sword made by a mortal. The faery folk could not be seen to seek their help nor ask for it. So when you came down into the cavern it was a gift that set off a chain of events leading to your father making the silver sword necessary to defeat the evil stoorworm.'

Loth and the daughter found their way back to the blacksmith's cottage in Gilmerton and were greeted with tears of joy. From then on, the blacksmith made sure that the trapdoor to the cavern below was never accessed again and what lay beneath was left undisturbed for many, many years.

7

JIMMY BORTHWICK'S BATTLE

Nanny B carefully put the album on the table. It was big and dusty with that particular type of musty smell that you get with old things. Each page contained photographs pasted onto thick scrapbook paper with crisp but delicate leaves of tissue in between. Carefully she unfastened the album's catch. As it creaked open, her faced widened with a warm smile, the kind you would wear to greet an old friend. The first picture was black and white, faded and blurry. A formal family photograph, women and children primly seated, father standing stiffly to the side. All eyes to the front, no smiles, just strange expressions – as if trying to prevent the camera looking into their very souls. I craned my neck to get a better look.

Nanny B's crooked finger slowly traced across the line of faces as she said each name out loud, her mouth savouring the names, trying them out for size, remembering them respectfully. There were seven all told, each bearing some form of resemblance to either the father or mother. The square-set chin, the way the hair curled, the high cheekbones. I had often heard Nanny B talk about these people, my relatives, mythical ancestors, all gone now. But their memories, their deeds, lived on through her stories of and about them.

Tenderly she turned each page, pausing now and then to comment or merely bask in reveries. Towards the end of the album was one wee drawing on faded yellowing paper, an illustration of a severe-looking man with big sideburns and huge whiskers. His eyes were cold and discerning, the kind of eyes belonging to a man who does not compromise and has an exacting nature.

'Who is that guy?' I said.

'That was my great-great-grandad, Jimmy Borthwick. It's a good likeness but the picture doesn't do him justice. He lived to the ripe old age of ninety-three. Was still fit and mentally active up until the day he died.'

'He looks so stern.'

'Auch, don't let that fool you. He was the life and soul of the party, a real character. Did you know that he was the youngest of thirteen children and the only boy? The apple of his mother's eye so he was; spoiled rotten too.'

'Why is he wearing that cap? Was he in the army?'

'No, that's a railwayman's cap. You see the badge? It was a big deal back then to get a job with the North British Railway. You only got it if the Board approved of you. "All employees must be of robust health, good character and not exceeding the age of forty," he would tell us frequently. He would straighten his back and square his shoulders as he said it. Like this.' She made to stand upright, jutting her chin out with her nose in the air.

'They were very strict and competition for the jobs was fierce. When on duty a porter had to wear the company badge bearing his number,' she said in an affected low voice. 'But to obtain the badge he had to pay the sum of ten shillings for the privilege. That was a lot of money back then. He got the porter job when the line eventually opened up.'

'What do you mean "eventually"?'

'Well, the railway wasn't always here. Before that, everything was transported by horse and cart. The railway in Gorebridge only started up in 1832 and that was on account of the Marquis of

Lothian wanting to transport his coal from the mines in Arniston to Edinburgh.'

Nanny B had a head for facts, always had the year and names as well as the story. She was a bit like a history book all of her own.

'Then, in 1845, the North British Railway bought the line off the marquis and started to expand it. The new railway development put an end to the old way of life, making things quicker, more efficient. Old Jimmy even helped lay the new lines too; working as a navvie for Messers Graham and Sandison. There were two rival firms that employed navvies; Wilson and Moore was the other one. They were divided by nationality and religious belief. If you were Protestant and either Scottish or English you went with Graham and Sandison. If you were Catholic and Irish, you went with the other. Occasionally old Jimmy would have one too many whiskies then he would get all riled up about the "Fenians". He didn't like the Irish right up until his last breath.'

'I don't understand. Why was that?'

'Well,' Nanny B sucked in her breath and glanced at the drawing of Jimmy, 'back in those days I think folk were feared of anything different to the norm. It's a bit like some of the old attitudes with the football – if you aren't part of us you're against us. Tolerance wasn't in folks' make-up then. Course, the riot didn't help things.'

'Riot? What riot?'

'Did you not know? There was a riot here back in 1846. But to see how it happened … You need to understand that things were very different in those days. People were very narrow-minded, rigid in their attitudes. So, the riot happened because of these two factions of navvies. They had to be kept separate, work the lines at different times and places or else a stooshie would break out. They even lived in completely distinct areas, though on reflection I think the Irish had it harder. You know, they lived in huts? And they were sharing them with other families, or other single men, on the outskirts of Gorebridge.'

'Tell me more about the riot, Nanny B.'

'Wait a minute, son, patience. Where was I? Ah, yes, so according to Jimmy it all started in a spit-and-sawdust pub in Gorebridge. It was a cold Saturday afternoon, the end of the month. Pay day. The Irish had poured into it after work; it was probably the only warm place where they could all meet up.

'So the story goes that a salesman took some watches into that pub hoping to make a sale. They were passed about, but by all accounts the watches weren't of the best quality. Some folk, perhaps a little worse for wear and looser with their tongues than normal, commented. But the salesman got defensive and, well, he soon found himself the centre of attention. The mood changed from banter to malice. The salesman demanded his watches back, but the room went quiet and they all turned their heads away from him and refused to talk. The salesman left red-faced and empty-handed only to return a little later with the local police. Two Irishman were arrested and taken off to the local lock-up. You might think that it would have stopped there, but no: incensed by the police's actions their friends planned a break-out.

'About one o'clock on Sunday morning one hundred and fifty to two hundred of them took to the quiet streets of Gorebridge, and, walking six abreast up Main Street, made their way to the police lock-up. The lock-up was always in the middle of town, it's where the bank is now, you know, the one on the High Street?

'Well, there were only two policemen on watch at the time. They tried to quell the mob but things got nasty. They were overwhelmed by the sheer numbers. One of the labourers had a pistol, and the sergeant was attacked by someone wielding the back of an axe. Needless to say, they released the prisoners. Stirred with the sense of victory, the mob paraded their freed comrades through the streets, gallus and having a right carry-on, so they were.

'Unfortunately, two other constables who had been making the rounds saw the mob heading their way and, feart, decided to hide behind a hedge. They were spotted and a cry went out to "Murder the police!". Outnumbered again, and with nowhere to run, one policeman was knocked to the ground and savagely beaten, while the other received some major injuries but managed to get away.'

'What happened then?' I held my breath.

'Unfortunately the policeman who was knocked to the ground died. A deputation of county police and representatives from the Irish firm Wilson and Moore went out to Fushie Bridge, where the Irish navvies worked, to try and find the ringleaders. Thirteen of them were lifted for taking part in breaking open the lock-up. They were taken to jail in Edinburgh.

'By the Monday morning the news had travelled round the Protestant navvies and they wanted blood. Over a thousand of them mustered at Lothian Bridge, joined by some of the miners from the Marquis of Lothian's pits. All were armed – an assortment of weapons – pick-shafts, bludgeons and spade handles. They formed a procession and marched on Fushie Bridge. Seeing such a large force of angry people coming for them, the Irish took off, scattering all over the countryside.

'The mob felt they'd failed to achieve "justice" the crowd decided to burn the huts the Irish lived in, starting at Crichton Moor, right up to Borthwick Castle and beyond. The police were present, but there weren't enough of them to take on such an angry mob of that size, so they stood back and let them get on with it (though I suspect their loyalties lay with their countrymen).

A troop of Irish Dragoons had been sent for but by the time they arrived at five o'clock that afternoon, all the damage had been done and those responsible were safely home behind locked doors. Later that evening, the police and dragoons arrested nineteen people for burning the huts and took *them* to jail in Edinburgh, too.'

'So, was Jimmy Borthwick involved in the riot?'

'Not according to his mother. Apparently she went to her grave believing that he was asleep in his bed and knew nothing about it. But Jimmy's story was altogether different. He says it was the sound of the tackety-boots marching down the road that woke him the night of the murder. Said he watched them making "a show of themselves", as they paraded down the street, full of the drink and mischief. On the Monday he and his father tried to join the throng but Jimmy's mother boxed their ears and dragged them back home; made them stay home and polish the range to within an inch of its life. Now she was a force to be reckoned with.'

'What happened in the end?'

'Well, by all accounts, after the dragoons had taken the nineteen people to jail, the Irish started to assemble around the Cowgate in Edinburgh itself, with the specific intent of "paying back the Scotchmen, with interest". As their numbers swelled they made their way along the main road up to Dalkeith but were met by the sheriff and members of the constabulary. It took a lot of persuading to get them to think about what they were doing and turn back. Jimmy said it was a close-run thing.

'There were some more arrests for the burning of the huts, thirty, I think, in total, and that's not including those jailed for the riot. Both firms employing the navvies responded swiftly. Between them they fired one hundred and fifty labourers for their part in the riot. I bet you'll think again when you say nothing happens around here won't you, son?'

'Aye, that I will Nanny B.'

She smiled and carefully closed the album on the stern face of Jimmy Borthwick, my great-great-great-grandad.

This story came to me quite by accident; a passing comment by someone in a chip shop! I eventually tracked the information down in the Gorebridge Yesterdays 1989 *magazine.*

8

How Holyrood
Came to Be

The following story is an old story, passed down through the centuries, which has now taken on legendary status. The arms of the Canongate, a district of Edinburgh founded by King David I, contain an image of a white doe. It serves to maintain the legend of how Holyrood came to be, or, as it was known in the old Scots at the time, Haly Rood, or Holy Cross.

The cross is also a significant aspect of the story as it is claimed that the 'holy cross' came from far afield; made of the finest ebony it had, hidden deep within its black wood a sliver of the wood from the Cross upon which Christ himself was crucified.

This Holy Cross found its way to Scotland with Margaret, the mother of King David I. Her arrival was quite by happenstance.

As a young princess she and her family fled the ravages of William the Conqueror who overthrew the Saxon Kings of England during the Battle of Hastings. They boarded a boat bound for Europe but a storm blew it off course and they ended up in the Firth of Forth.

The young Margaret went on to marry the King of Scots, Malcolm Canmore. She was devoutly religious and her gentle pious ways had a positive, calming influence on the king. On her deathbed it is said that she held in her hands the venerated relic of the Haly Rood. It was some years after her death that David took the throne of Scotland.

One fine autumn day in the year 1127, preparations in Edinburgh castle were well under way for the celebration of the Feast of the Holy Cross. Beyond the castle walls the breath of the dawn morning was still lying low on the ground. Harebells trembled as the bloodhound padded past, leaving deep paw prints in the soft mud. Occasionally it strained on the leash, its attendant, a valet de limer of the highest calibre named John Joe, hauling hard to keep up but not so hard as to prevent play. Every now and then this bloodhound, a lime-hound would stop, nose to the floor, haver a moment or two, picking up the scent, then lunge on, ears a-flapping.

John Joe urged him on in low half-whispered tones, 'On boy. Go. Seek. Find me a stag.' Onwards they stumbled, over paths criss-crossed with fallen logs green with moss, a tumble of autumn leaves, bracken, gorse and small animal tracks.

Then, quite suddenly, the dog halted, stock still. John Joe stopped in unison with the hound and turned his head to follow the dog's gaze. At first he didn't see anything. It was as though the light and the trees had conspired against him, shielding their secret. Gradually his eyes adjusted. It was there, revealed before him, just beyond the evergreens, quietly grazing: a stag, sporting the most spectacular rack of antlers that he had ever seen.

John Joe barely managed to stop himself from gasping out loud. His heart boomed so noisily in his chest that it occurred to him that even the stag might hear. This was a magnificent beast by any standard; mature, impressively charismatic and carrying more than ten points on its antlers. But best of all, it was a white hart. The white hart of mythical renown and much sought after.

Slowly John Joe crouched down among the ferns beneath the shadows of the forest trees and waited. He watched in silent awe, hardly daring to breathe. The hart moved with grace and purpose, as if aware of its supreme beauty. There was power in this creature, not just in its physicality but something else that John Joe couldn't quite fathom. He had been involved in many a hunt before now and so knew what was expected and what was to come; he had tracked many a stag in his time, but this animal superseded all other experiences. It was different in a manner that he couldn't quite express and not solely because it was the 'white hart'.

He loved this aspect of his work, questing. He was in the unique position to witness sights such as this, untrammelled by conventions of conduct or social standing for John Joe was a valet de limer, just as his father had been before him. It was a prestigious position that carried much responsibility and status amongst his peers but to John Joe the beauty lay in being left to his own devices. Nature would take its own course; he merely needed to pay attention to the hound and the movements of the quarry. It was vital that the nobles had a good hunt and finding a warrantable stag such as this lent itself to the hunting party's success.

He watched the hart move off, mentally noting which direction and marking the spot with a small pile of stones, safe in the knowledge that the tracks would do the rest of the work. Then he made his way back to the lodge in double-quick time. The hunt was on.

By the time he had returned to the castle, Mass and prayers had already taken place in observance of the religious occasion. When the king received word of the valet's find there followed a flurry of activity. Despite the protestations of the priests and bishops – 'This is unseemly on such a holy day' – the king was determined to hunt. After all, was not the presence of a white hart significant too?

Soon the running hounds were ready, the horses quickly saddled and mounted. They paced with graceful arching necks, stamping and sidestepping with anticipation. A great sense of excitement and expectation ran through the castle as word of the mythical white hart was carried on the lips of the king, his nobles, retainers and stable boys alike. Before long, horses carrying the hunting party thundered out midst a flutter of banners and flags, hooves clattering on the cobblestones as they made their way out through the gates at the Netherbow and Cannongate and on out into the forest beyond. Wild foxgloves waved their clustering bells as they passed. Running dogs barked and yelped, falcons trussed in jesses worried and flapped, their tinkling bells ringing softly above the din. Far off, in the depths of the forest, an occasional horn sounded, its note virtually swallowed into the depths beyond, seemingly absorbed by swathing mists. The autumn-dressed trees had closed in on themselves, muting the sounds to quickly restore a restful quiet.

Just as the early morning light began to blend from silver to pink and gold, a doe and her fawn appeared, stepping out of the trees into a small glade. They stopped to nibble on a small tassel of grass illuminated by the weak sunshine. The doe, graceful but solicitous, kept a watchful eye, her ears flicking back and forth as she honed in on the sounds. Above, crows cawed and flapped, greeting the morning with fractious cries as creatures scurried and scampered on the leafy forest floor below.

An hour, maybe two passed without much event. The doe and her fawn had long moved on to drink in the pools of black water found in secret parts of the wood.

A shout, followed by a chorus of voices, filled the air. Horses neighed, brasses jangled as hooves pounded the forest floor leaving behind the odours of resin, mouldering leaves, leather and horse sweat in their wake. The cries grew louder as the retinue sallied forth. The hunt was in full swing.

A boar crashed out of the undergrowth in an effort to escape. Its ears flattened to the back of its head as its legs worked at speed. Its squeals grew louder and more agitated as the horses gained on their quarry. It wasn't long before the arrow hit its mark. The stricken animal attempted to crawl into the gorse, squealing, its breath laboured and broken, before receiving the final death blow.

After, when the entrails had been removed, and the unmaking completed, the dogs fought and scrapped over their rewards while the slaughtered boar's fore and aft legs were tied together, attached to a stick and ferried back to the castle.

The hunt continued; this time the hart's scent and trail had been picked up. The dogs were set in relay as the nobles charged on. For a while horses and dogs crashed around the forest hard on the stag's trail. It proved to be cunning and elusive, providing only fleeting glimpses, springing and darting out of sight.

The horses began to tire. Their withers covered in sweaty foam and nostrils flaring as they drew breath. Just at the point where it was felt that the stag had managed to give the hunt the slip, something uncanny happened. The stag darted out, right before the king, stopping to look back momentarily then speeding off. The king spurred his horse on, leaving the rest of the hunt behind and disappearing into the depths of the forest.

Emerging out of a thicket into a small clearing, the king suddenly found himself face to face with the stag. He had it at bay. The stag stood still, breathing deeply, its lungs, like barrels, expanding and contracting. Its presence was enough to unsettle the king's horse. Suddenly it shied, rearing up on its hind legs, virtually unseating him. He leaned forward, gripping on to the mane with his hands and sitting low into the saddle.

'Woa, steady, steady.' He spoke in hushed tones in an effort to calm the steed and take control. Under different circumstances it would have been the perfect position for a shot but the horse was too frightened.

Kicking hard with his heels the king tried to urge the horse forward, but the terrified animal reared up again, pawing with its front legs. It whinnied, showing the whites of its eyes. The king tumbled to the floor leaving the horse to gallop off, its reins trailing at its hooves.

The king was barely back on his feet when the huge beast began snorting and stamping its feet. It tossed its head back and forth, displaying its impressive rack of antlers. The king was transfixed.

Fear and awe rooted him to the spot. For a moment it seemed as though they recognised each other – monarchs of their own domains. The forest fell eerily silent.

A beam of sunlight filtered through the trees to illuminate the area where the hart and the king stood. Slowly the hart began to paw the ground, then, with the fullness of its might, charged headlong towards the king.

The hunting party, sitting some way off, could only imagine what was happening. They saw the king's horse appear full canter without a rider. They could hear the thud and scrape of hooves and the rustle of leaves. But, as if spellbound, could only sit and listen to the event unfold in the glade beyond.

The king had to act quickly if he wanted to survive being gored. He stood, motionless, arms at his side, ready and primed to receive the stag. He watched as the antlers advanced, bearing down on him at speed. He braced himself. Just at the point of contact, a bright light in the shape of the Cross lit up between the stag's horns.

In that fleeting moment the king was convinced that it was a sign from God.

Startled, the beast's hind legs buckled as he stretched out his forelegs in an effort to stop short. Barely three feet separated them. Both remained rigid. They looked each other in the eye, breathing hard. In a bound, the stag about turned and sprang away, off into the depths of the forest. The waiting retinue caught a brief glimpse of the stag, its tail flashing as it swiftly disappeard from sight.

The king fell to his knees, put his hands together and prayed fervently. When he arose, he announced to all that he had made a solemn pledge to the Lord. He would mark the spot where divine intervention had saved his life. King David decided to build an abbey as a way of paying tribute to this event.

A year later, Holyrood Abbey was founded on the site where the miracle took place and so-named to mark the 'place of the holy cross'.

9

THE GALLOPING HORSEMAN OF PENICUIK

This tale is well known among the locals from Penicuik, harking back to the day when the lime works were in operation. Hardly a trace of it is left now but the memory of the ghost lives on ...

The nightshift workers had not long clocked on, filing in slowly and selecting tools such as hammers, mallets, chisels or trowels with careful, considered diligence. Most of the workers who had been at the job a long time brought their own tools, something reliable and sturdy.

Dust was not a lime worker's friend but was a major facet of the job. It got everywhere, eyes, ears, nose, hair – every crevice possible. You could tell a lime worker easily: they were the ones covered in a film of white dust, leaving trails of footsteps and markings everywhere they went.

The men looked strange; like the walking dead, some said. They had an eerie kind of glow against the background of the quarry walls and the light from the glowing lanterns. To an outsider they looked like phantoms, their forms throwing long flickering shadows around the walls, moving to the steady thump and clang of mallet and chisel on stone.

Above ground, where the air was fresh, all that could be heard was the rhythmic tapping and the occasional cough and spit.

James hadn't long been with the company. It was his first job and he had been taken on as an apprentice. Still young and impressionable, he was assigned to work with Bill Jennings, an old hand with over thirty years' skill and experience to share. It was said that what he didn't know about the trade wasn't worth knowing. James had been assured that he would be in good hands working alongside him. Although fast coming up for retirement, Bill still had the grit and mettle of men half his age; he could easily last a twelve-hour shift without tiring but he could be hard, showing little sympathy for struggling novices.

That evening James had turned up for the shift early as advised. His mother had packed his piece and something to drink, chiding him not to eat too early as it would be a long night and it was best to keep a little back. She tried desperately not to fuss; sadness did not allow her hands to be idle.

The old routine of making up a piece for her husband from years back returned with ease but it also reopened that chasm of grief. The same quarry had taken Jim, her husband, twenty years before, when James was still a toddler. She would have given anything to avoid James following his father's footsteps but the more she protested the more he determined to tread the same path.

Bill stood at the gate where he had been waiting and welcomed James with a vice-like handshake, his rough hands the size of shovels, calloused and ingrained with limestone. 'Good to see you, son,' he said in a raspy voice. Then he stood back a little to look at him. His rheumy white eye, static in its socket, had an unnerving quality about it making James shift from foot to foot and look uncomfortably to the ground.

'You're the spit of your father.' There followed a strained pause. 'Stay close and listen carefully, I'll keep you right and, more importantly, I'll keep you safe.'

James nodded in acknowledgement yet continued to stare fixedly at the floor.

Although relatively small in stature Bill was broad of shoulder and strong as an ox. He knew instinctively how best to hew difficult pieces of lime from the rock face, even jested saying he'd been doing the job so long he could do it with his good eye closed. Watching him toil, James was convinced it was probably true. The work had taken its toll, though: Bill had lost the sight in one eye, and part of his face and left arm were scarred and pocked from working with the lime, but he was one of the lucky ones; he was still alive.

Several hours passed. Bill showed James the subtle nuances of being a lime burner; he worked the rock with ease, knowing precisely where to land the hammer and which angle to hold the chisel to make the rock surrender her gems. It was pure joy to behold a master craftsman at his work.

They had stopped to take a rest, as Bill's breathing had become rather laboured, his lungs working like bellows as he coughed and spat to draw breath.

They sat a little away from the mouth of the quarry on upturned buckets, looking up at the stars in the dark night sky. Suddenly a bird flew out of a thicket, fluttering its wings and squawking in protest as it went. Bill touched James lightly on the arm.

'Hold still lad, wheesht. Lest he kens we're here.'

They sat motionless, hunkered over the buckets for what seemed like an age. Then, against the background noise of the quarry, James heard a soft, distant thrumming sound, like fingers drumming on wood. It became louder and clearer as it got closer to them. Whatever it was, it was definitely heading towards them at some speed – a rhythmic pounding of galloping hooves. They both looked up and watched, taken aback by the sight of a strange ghostly horse and its charge hurtling along the road, heading south towards Peebles.

'Holy Mother of … Did you see that, Bill?'

Bill remained tight-lipped, staring out into the blackest black of the sky.

'He comes every night – and he'll be along again shortly. Not everyone sees or hears him, just a few. Your father was one of them.'

'But what, who, is it Bill?' Fear had crept into James' voice and gave away his tender years.

'Too many questions for now, son, we best get back to work.'

James could barely concentrate; his mind raced at lightning speed, making it difficult to settle on anything. Fear and curiosity make an unlikely pair. He also wanted to make a good impression so fought hard to quell his anxiety and focus; after all, one false move and the outcome could be fatal.

What had his father thought of the strange sight? Had he ever mentioned it to his mother? Did she know anything about this?

Lunchtime soon rolled around. Bill and James took out their pieces and made their way back to the buckets; again Bill's laboured breath was quite pronounced. A few of the other lime workers joined them, drifting off to various corners to smoke, play cards or eat. They looked a strange sight covered head to foot in grey-white, giving the impression of ragged figures hewn from marble.

James took his time before broaching the subject of the phantom-like figure witnessed earlier. He sensed that it was a touchy subject but for his own part couldn't leave it alone. He wasn't sure if he would be able to continue working there if he didn't understand it, or at least have some information to help him understand. Bill looked rather uncomfortable at first, then, clenching his jaw and clearing his throat, he began.

'It is said that there was once a farm in Eddleston. It was situated just along this road, the Peebles Road. A lass worked there as a bondager, working with the hind and his family to help around the farm. She was a bonny lass from all accounts, caught many the heart of the young men around here. Eventually she took up with a young ploughman who lived and worked out this way.

The story goes he visited the lass as often as he could by stealing away out on the fleetest of his master's horses and galloping down to Eddleston to see her of an evening. It all sounded very romantic and from what I was told, he was truly smitten with her.

Then one night, as he neared the limekilns, he came upon a cart laden with wood. Something had happened. The horse had been startled and had bolted. The driver, although having many years' experience of working driving carts, had been unable to wrestle back control as the horse charged blindly ahead without heed to the road or driver. Seemingly they ended up in the ditch with the cart and contents overturned. The driver found himself beneath the cart and had been badly injured, his horse unable to move as it had broken its leg.

As the young ploughman approached, the carter cried pitifully for help but the young man turned a blind eye, choosing instead to ride on to meet his young lass.

When he returned a couple of hours later the carter was still there, lying in the ditch cold and in pain and obviously mortally wounded. Again the cart driver cried out, pleading with the young ploughman to help him. This time the ploughman was anxious to return the horse back to his master's stable. He feared his master's reaction should he be caught with the horse without permission. It would have put paid to his nightly trysts and probably lost him his job. So he chose, yet again, to ignore the wounded man's cries and instead of stopping to help, spurred the horse on, speeding off into the blackness of the night.

'Now, Penicuik was once a small town and every face was well kent and so the carter recognised the young ploughman but didn't know him by name. By the time morning came, lime workers heading out to the quarry came across the injured carter pinned to the floor by the cart's load. They worked quickly to release him and as they lifted his limp and near-dead body from beneath the load he roused himself, living long enough to tell of the young ploughman who had ignored him and refused to help.

The story sparked a great sense of outrage and shame among the lime workers who in turn spread the news throughout the countryside. It travelled like wildfire and very soon the account was on the lips of every household in Penicuik and beyond.

It did not take long for folk to figure out who exactly the young ploughman was. He was shunned at the kirk and market. No one spoke to him, turning their backs whenever he appeared. He lost his job on the farm, his girlfriend jilted him, saying quite resolutely that she would rather see him in hell than have anything more to do with him.

'Dejected and isolated, the young ploughman was both desperate and depressed. He took himself away out into the countryside, carrying his hunting gun with him. At the time, poaching among ploughmen was commonplace, so we can't be sure whether the young man took his own life or accidentally shot himself while poaching. Needless to say, he was found dead some days later.

A shepherd came across him lying in the woods; his eyes pecked out by carrion. They took his body to the local mortuary and it was left there for a while. The locals couldn't decide what to do with him, they argued back and forth. You see, his actions had riled and offended local people so much that in the end they refused to bury him in consecrated ground.

Eventually it was decided that his remains should be buried at the point where the lands of the three lairds met – Firth, Whitehall and Rosebery, and a paling stake be driven through his body for good measure.

So, even to this day if a bird is heard flying away, startled by the night, or a muircock is heard to cry out in the dark hours, just like

we heard earlier, there are those who would say that it was flushed
out by the ghost of the galloping horseman.'

Just as Bill was finishing off the tale the faint rhythmic sound of
hooves could be heard, only this time coming from the direction
they had sped off to earlier, signifying the horse and rider's return
journey. As it got closer to the quarry, both horse and rider were
seen to take a leap high into the air while at the same time issuing a
terrible bloodcurdling scream.

In that moment James thought his heart would stop from fear.
He turned to look Bill full in the face, rheumy eye and all. He see
read no fear in his features but merely an unreadable expression,
eyes staring forward in resignation.

'Course, you must know now that you should never, under any
circumstances, walk that road alone at night.'

James sat rigid, barely able to utter a word.

'He knows you now. You've seen his face. He'll come after you,
mark my words. Come lad, best we get back to work. We'll no get
paid for sitting around out here wondering about the horseman.'

*A big thank you to Linda Early, artist, sculptress and fabulous
dressmaker, who kindly told me this tale on a cold winter's night beside
a blazing fire.*

10

CAMP MEG OF
MAYFIELD

The first time I ever saw Meg was at Dalkeith. They were holding
a horserace on the day of the Feeing Fayre. In she rode on this grey
cob, must have stood all of fifteen hands. Skewbald she called it.

You couldn't miss her: carried herself like a man and looked a
bit like one too. Nothing seemed to faze her; the children taunted
her, folk laughed behind her back. She treated everyone the same,
friendly but distant.

All the farmers knew her too; they would catch her eye and
nod as she passed by. The kind of nod that conferred great
respect, and that was hard to get without hard graft and skill in
the farm work.

I remember all the nay-sayers who didn't really know her,
standing about waiting for the race to begin and all being shocked-
affronted that a woman was entering into it. Tongues were really
wagging that day.

Well, bless my soul if Meg didn't go and win the race. No sooner
was the signal given to go than she set off at full speed, virtually
leaving the rest of them standing. By the time she came past the
finish line she was greeted with rousing cheers and whoops of joy.

Sally, I said to myself, that is one person you just have to get to
know. She was so different and yet indifferent at the same time.

When I asked about her I was always met with the same responses. It seemed there was nothing to tell.

No one in Mayfield really knew where she came from. There were those who were quick to cast doubt and suspicion, standing in their doorways, shawls tightly drawn around their shoulders. It was the huddle and the occasional look behind them; the conspiratorial gap in conversation that gave them away. Gossips. They just couldn't help themselves.

They called her all kinds of names but mostly they called her a witch. Some said she had the ability to be in two places at one time. Old Mrs Fairbairn swore she saw her in the wood gathering sticks, yet when she looked in through the cottage window, said she saw her in there too. Not that I believe it, as she mistook Mr Cummins for her husband with only six feet between them. Now that stands her lies on their head, doesn't it?

Meg gave those gossips ample material to work with. She appeared out at the camp on the edge of D'Arcy farm early one spring some twenty years ago. Kept herself very much to herself, closed and self-contained, with little time for the likes of them.

They say she rode in on that sturdy cob, head held high despite the fact that her hair was matted. She wore a vest, trousers and wellingtons beneath that greatcoat, God forbid! It made her look older than her twenty-something years. At her side trotted her wee dog, never took its eyes off her. She called it Help, a stumpy wee thing, short legs, three white socks, long tail with a curl at its tip and a head too big for its body. Looked as though it housed enough teeth to put the devil to shame. It seemed biddable enough but no one wanted to risk clapping it to find out. Wherever Meg went you could guarantee that her wee dog was not far behind.

As for Meg, she was a larger-than-life character once you got to know her. Her voice carried but her laughter carried much further, long after she had left. It was a good hearty laugh, the kind that embraced you in its warmth and coaxed you into an irresistible chuckle that soon lent itself to a full-blown belly laugh. And whether it was Meg or her laughter, you always felt all the better for seeing her. All the farmers respected her highly. Not for her looks – you wouldn't have called her a bonny lass – but for her knowledge. What she didn't know about the stock or horses, especially the horses, wasn't worth knowing.

When John Forsyth's cows went down with the barking cough and fever, all the other farms around thought that Forsyth's stock would be 'ripe for diggin in'. Labourers and stockmen made ready for a mass culling. Then Meg appeared, no one stopped to ask where from. Apparently she just rode up to Forsyth's land when all the others were giving it a wide berth.

Calmly she dismounted Skewbald, tied the reins, went across the paddock and climbed over the gate, surprisingly nimble for her size.

The animals were in a sorry state by then, lying on their sides, coughing, panting and bloated, unable to struggle to their feet. Gently she spoke to each of them, checked their eyes, the colour of their swollen tongues. She felt their bellies and, as if reassured she knew what it was she was dealing with, she then fed them a treacle-like substance. It stank of mould and dank water, brackish in colour. The animals lay still for an hour or two after, closing their eyes to the flies that buzzed around them. Meg stayed close at hand and every hour on the hour she followed the same routine. By the morning, every one of the stock was standing on its feet, feebly swishing their tails and stamping their hooves.

The animals had shifted from death's door to health overnight thanks to Meg. That was when they first heard her infectious laugh, proper head thrown back, throat exposed to the sky, deep and throaty. Forsyth, my master, was overjoyed – tried to push coins into her palm but she refused, wanting nothing more than a bite to eat, food for her animals and a safe piece of land to bide.

Forsyth let her have Warston House, that old tumbledown cottage situated among the woods above D'Arcy Farm. It had once

been used as a station to warn people of the French invasion during the Napoleonic Wars and, prior to that, a Roman Camp. Now everyone called it The Camp. It was remote, but that suited both of them. After that, it didn't matter what the folk had to say about her, good or bad, Meg had her own place. The farmers would see that she stayed; they needed her skills and know-how.

It wasn't long before she earned herself the name 'Cattle Doctor' and soon she was holding surgeries in Penicuik on Tuesdays, Dalkeith on Thursdays and Haddington on Fridays. She even got the respect of the bi-annual Caledonian Hunt; they played on her reputation to be able to frighten the children and used her to keep the unruly youngsters out of the hunt path. They even organised a special collection for her before the start of each of the hunts. That was more powerful than idle gossip and hearsay.

As the years passed I got to know Meg better. She didn't talk much about herself, but once told me that her father was a horseman from somewhere down in the Borders.

Maybe that was where she learnt her horse skills. Some claimed she must have known about The Horseman's Word, that secret society that knew all about horses. 'Hide, heal, never reveal' was their mantra. That magic, that knowledge, belonged to the world of men, and some would say they were in league with the deil himself. But Meg didn't fit into that, surely? Aye, she had a sense of humour – when she knew the children were lurking round the camp she would make out she hadn't seen them and start chanting weird words, 'Talla, tall, ada, daum, da' or something like that. I actually watched her one day; she winked at me as she did it. Then she said in a loud voice, 'The devil visits me regularly here at The Camp, face as old as the hills and is red and blue in colour.' The children soon scarpered, leaving us bent double with laughter.

One time, as I was heading up to The Camp, a wee tune popped into my head. It reminded me of my Dumfries granny, of howkin tatties and picking berries out in the fields. There was always a song to accompany farm work and she, being a bondager like myself, knew plenty. So there I was singing 'Oh the Gallawa hills are covered wi' broom' when out of nowhere Meg joined in. She stood there beaming, her greatcoat flapping in the wind, and gave it her all. We sang all the way to her house. Yet I sensed a wistfulness when she told me she hadn't heard that song in a long while.

Her house was sparse, tree stumps for a table and seats. With soup puckering on the range, I began to tell her about my Dumfries granny, the farm she worked, the people she knew. Then Meg grew still and ashen-faced.

'Her name was Bella, wasn't it?' she said.

The silence was crushing. I nodded slowly, unable to lift my eyes. But Meg needed to speak, needed to be heard for the first time in years.

Her story tumbled from her lips, gradually picking up speed and pace as she talked. She painted vivid pictures, used turns of phrases only found around my granny's folk. I learned that she grew up under *my* granny's watchful eye.

Her mother had died and granny Bella was taken on as a bondager, all farmers insisted on having a bondager working with the ploughman back then.

As she told her story, it reminded me of the stories my granny used to tell about the farm. Stories I thought were just that, stories.

Granny would sit me on her knee and tell us the 'Maggie stories'. We loved those best of all. We begged her to tell us them over and over again.

Maggie, or Margaret Hawthorn as she was formerly known, was a spirited character, one that my sisters and I could relate to because she was a girl and a gallus one too; we would spend hours re-enacting the scenarios, especially the romance with the wealthy landowner followed by a decadent wedding.

It seemed like she had it all with the birth of a son, but the happiness was to be short-lived. The wealthy landowner died quite suddenly.

My sisters and I would fight over who got to play that part. Such delight in falling down dramatically clutching at the heart for my then eight-year-old self.

Then followed the duel between Maggie and the evil neighbour. We all wanted to play the heroine, fending off the vile bad man. Of course, we didn't fully understand why he was deemed so bad, but had this notion that it had something to do with land.

It was in that moment it dawned on me that Meg and Maggie were more than likely one and the same person.

'Did you really shoot your neighbour?' The words came out before I could stop myself.

Meg's mouth twisted, she flattened her palms on the table and nodded her head. 'Yes,' she whispered. 'And I would do it again if I had to.'

I could have sworn I saw her lip curl as she said it. She held her head up and jutted out her chin defiantly. Her dog, sensing her mood had changed, got up from where he lay and put his big muckle head in her lap.

In a faltering voice Meg explained that after her husband's sudden death her neighbour began a campaign against her, claiming that her land belonged to him. He took her to court and took her for every penny she had. She struggled to cope with a young child.

When the neighbour came on to her land shouting and threatening all sorts, something came over her. The pistol was there, in her hands. Next thing she knew there was a bang and he was lying on the ground, dead.

Panic-stricken she ran, leaving her son with a trusted friend, and that was the last she ever saw or heard of him.

Meg made me promise never to tell a soul of this and until this very day I have never uttered a word.

I heard tell that years later her son found her up at The Camp. He begged her to return back to Gallaway with him and be reunited with family and old friends.

I suspect it was her sense of shame that prevented her from letting him cross her threshold. The child that she had given up didn't know; the nature of her living circumstances being so vastly different to that of the young man that stood before her. They were worlds apart now.

Meg, as we knew her, continued to live and work in Mayfield, helping with the health of the livestock and horses until a ripe old age. Then one severe winter in 1872 Meg was found dead on her doorstep covered in snow. The whole of Mayfield responded and clubbed together to pay for her funeral; she was well liked by many of the Esk Valley folk too. Finally they had claimed her as one of theirs.

Her funeral took place at the graveyard at Newbattle Old Cemetery. As it turned out Meg had been canny and had sold her body to a Mr Laidlaw for twenty shillings, just a year prior to her death, on condition that it would be used for medical research and he bury what was left of her remains beneath the large hawthorn tree near her house with the following inscription:

Caledonia's huntsmen now safely may scamp,
Since their heroine's gone, the pride of their camp.
Her bones are at rest now, her soul's on the tramp,
In the valley of death thro' yon deep dreary swamp.
May she be guided safely thither by lamp – the lamp of Glory.

I have visited the camp and there is no evidence of a hawthorn tree or inscription but there is a gravestone commemorating Meg just near the wall in Newbattle Old Cemetery.

Even to this day Meg is still the subject of rumours, one of which states that the vast fortune that she accumulated from her extraordinary powers as a cattle doctor is still buried up in the woods to this day. The other claims she was a witch. But was she? I doubt it, just very skilled at working with animals and using some folk medicine as many have done before her time.

Camp Meg is a true local story – I collected many different versions from local people in and around the area. I also referred to Midlothian Local Studies Archives to confirm the facts.

11

HALF-HANGED MAGGIE

I am often in Musselburgh, a town which lies approximately six miles east of the city. From certain vantage points there are beautiful panoramic views of the coast of the Firth of Forth. When I look at its busy bustling streets, I often try to imagine how life must have been during particular times in the town's history.

The following story takes us back all the way to the early 1700s, a time when the wool and mining industries provided work for many of the local folk. There was also a large fishing community living down at the Fisherrow, near the harbour. This was home to a once vibrant community, strong in its ties and traditions. The work by its very nature was stark and harsh, and it is here that our story takes place.

In 1702 a certain Maggie Dickson was born to fisher folk in Fisherrow, Musselburgh. She was a raggedy wee thing, all elbows and knees with not an ounce of fat on her. Her hair hung in rats-tails beneath her scarf and her dark eyes looked as if they had been set with smudgy fingers.

She was the eldest of her mother's brood and didn't all the other ones know it. Bossy and cussed, quick of wit and sharp of tongue, she kept her siblings in line, taking on the role of the second mother, and had a set of lungs that could outcall even the best of the local fish hawkers.

As soon as she was old enough she was put to work alongside her mother and aunties. For the women, work began even before the fishermen's boats had left the harbour. Maggie quickly learned how to clean the lines (also known as redding) and attach mussels and buckie as bait. This skill required great care: one slip and a finger could be sliced. Once the fish had been brought to harbour and had been cleaned and gutted they then had to be sold.

Maggie's tiny frame bent as she helped to carry freshly caught fish into Edinburgh. Early mornings saw her disappearing up the street with quick heavy steps, off to sell her wares. She took to carrying the creel on her back at an earlier age than most, although this was not surprising given the number of mouths that needed feeding in her family household. Hunger and poverty were never far from their door.

The fishing was in her blood. Everyone in her family had something to do with it, from her daddy and uncles going out with the boats, to her grandma, mother and aunties. So it was of no surprise when she married a fisherman, indeed it was expected of her. There was nothing that really stood out about Maggie at this point; she made her life and living just the same as many others in her community.

Life changed radically for Maggie when her husband disappeared. It was totally unexpected and she didn't know what to make of it. Had he left her for another? Had he been press-ganged into the Royal Navy or perhaps taken a job with a fishing fleet elsewhere? Many offered their opinions and pity but Maggie wanted neither. With mounting bills and a sense of shame at being left alone she made the decision to leave and try and find work elsewhere.

Her travels led her to Kelso near the Scottish Borders, far away from the fishing community in Musselburgh. She found work with an innkeeper in exchange for basic lodgings. The work was physically arduous and required long hours but anything was better than poverty and destitution.

The innkeeper had a son of a similar age to Maggie. She was young, lonely and vulnerable. At first she tried hard to ignore the young man's attentions but the more he pressed her the more she was flattered. Besides, being abandoned after only three months of marriage had dealt a bitter blow. A betrayal she had not anticipated. Before long Maggie and the innkeeper's son became romantically involved. However, the romance had already soured before Maggie realised she was with child. Out of desperation she did her utmost to make sure that the innkeeper did not discover her circumstance. Ashamed and afraid of being instantly dismissed, she went to great lengths to conceal her condition.

Unfortunately the pregnancy did not go full term and the child was born prematurely. It was stillborn. She gave birth in secret in the squalor and darkness of the room she lodged in, biting down on a filthy rag, her body strained and convulsed with the contractions while she fixed her eye on the harvest moon that shone through the tiny window. Weak from the effort of birthing soundlessly and frightened by the outcome, she decided that she would tell no one of what had happened. After all, she had no funds to pay for a funeral. But what to do with the body?

She hadn't really thought about what would be done with the child had it lived. She decided to dispose of the body by putting it into the River Tweed – her thinking was that the waters would carry it away with the current and conceal its short-lived existence. Tenderly she wrapped the child in her shawl, slipped out of the inn and took it down to the riverbank. She stood a long while, clutching its little body to her chest as the river waters babbled past. Guilt and pain rendered her incapable of casting her dead child into the water, so she left it on the riverbank carefully hidden among some bushes.

Before the day had ended the little body was discovered and traced to Maggie. Police came to the inn and roughly escorted her away to the Edinburgh Tollbooth to await trial. She was charged with causing the death of her child based on questionable medical evidence that the child had been born alive. The court sentenced her to a public death by hanging, which was scheduled to take place in the Grassmarket on 2 September 1724.

The night before the execution Maggie shivered in a cold, dank prison cell. She had time to reflect on her life and make her peace with God. The guards came early the next morning to take her to the place of execution. A large crowd had gathered in the spitting rain.

As she climbed the steps to certain death she could see the faces of her family and friends among the throng. Her mother cried and wailed, clinging on to her father as he struggled to hold her up. Her name and crime were called out to the waiting crowd and a solemn solitary drum rolled as the hangman made good the rope. Maggie visibly shook as he placed the noose around her neck. Gently he tried to reassure her, 'Dinnae worry lass, I'll make it quick for you.' When the time came she recalled the sudden drop, the urgent struggle. Constriction and pain around her neck. Blackness.

Half an hour later, her limp body twisted in the breeze. The hangman and colleagues took her body down and pronounced her dead. The crowd became restless as members of Maggie's family and friends surged forward to surround and take possession of her. Arguments ensued as the family fought hard to retain the right to take her body home to bury. It was a simple request, that she be buried in her family's parish churchyard in Musselburgh. But another faction were also arguing for the body – medical students, eager for a fresh young cadaver to dissect and with a handsome purse to sway the hangman's judgement. Fortunately the family won out and Maggie's body was handed over and transferred to a cheap wooden coffin, which had been loaded onto the back of a cart.

The party of family and friends set off at a respectful pace and headed in the direction of Musselburgh. A couple of factors came into play to aid Maggie's spectacular resurrection during the journey home: firstly, the coffin was cheap but functional and as such let in air; secondly, the journey home entailed travelling along cobbled streets, jostling the cart and its contents. With the party mostly travelling by foot, progress would have been slow, mourners easily tired and more than likely hungry and in need of alcoholic sustenance. So, by all accounts, it stopped at a roadside inn near Peffermill to take some 'refreshments'.

By the time they reached the inn Maggie had been shuggled awake. She began knocking and banging in earnest until finally the lid was removed by the astonished party. Although weak, Maggie revived enough to climb out of her coffin. She walked the rest of the journey home to Musselburgh the next day.

The law took the view that as the sentence of the court had been carried out Maggie was beyond further prosecution; this was 'An Act of God' and as such she was free to go. The law also held that given Maggie had been executed, she was deemed dead in the eyes of the law and as such no longer married. Interestingly enough, while the king's advocate couldn't pursue her any further for her alleged crime, he did file a bill in the High Court of Justice against the sheriff for not ensuring that the punishment was appropriately carried out.

Maggie went on to live a further forty years. Her husband returned to the Fisherrow community and rekindled his relationship with Maggie, and, given that he was a man of good heart, married her again.

Over the years that followed she went on to have several more children and became a celebrity in her own right. Maggie became highly acclaimed to the people of Edinburgh and until the end of her days people would call out 'half-hanged Maggie' when she walked past them in the street.

As with all stories of this ilk, speculation abounds as to why she survived the hanging ordeal. I've heard tell that Maggie was very friendly with the rope maker who supplied the hangman, perhaps this could have had some bearing on the outcome? Whatever the reason, Maggie's story has passed into Edinburgh folklore and her name is remembered in the name of Maggie Dickson's Pub, which overlooks the scene of her 'execution' in Edinburgh's Grassmarket.

This is a well kent tale known by many local inhabitants. A more factual source for this true story can be found at the National Library of Scotland: A.P.S.4.98.8.

12

JENNY
LASSWADE

Lasswade is an exceptionally beautiful hamlet and parish in Midlothian situated in a picturesque dip where the North Esk River flows some nine miles south of Edinburgh city centre. Many of the locals know snippets of the legend of Jenny Lasswade, from which the area is said to have derived its name. A local inhabitant has captured the essence of the legend in a song. My take on the story offers an explanation as to how she came to this position in the first place.

JENNY LASSWADE

Jenny was a maiden from a village in Midlothian,
And she would carry gentlemen across a stream,
She put them on her shoulder for to wade across the water,
And they had tae pay her half way there or she would drop
    them in.
People came frae Dalkeith, Liberton and Gilmerton,
Frae Colinton and Roslin and Penicuik too,
They travelled in their carriages leading tae some marriages,
And when a come tae think of it I think I saw you.
She carried any maiden or a mannie that is laiden,
Wi' his instruments o tradin just as long as she wis paid,

And when the flow was heavy then she added tae her levy,
And the people shouted – 'ready steady Jenny Lasswade'.

Song by Ian McCalman
'Burn The Witch' (1978 Transatlantic TRA357)

A small dandelion seed lifted into the air and, spinning as though dancing to its own reel, floated out over the babbling river to slowly drift down to the North Esk water. Jenny, from her vantage point, situated just at the bend in the river where the water becomes a pool, watched this magical moment, the seed, to her, reminiscent of a wee faery. She had often imagined throngs of faeries playing gleefully among the bluebells and ferns that adorned the riverbank. She spent most of her days outside beneath the shade of the majestic chestnut trees, lying on her back looking up at the sky. She loved to watch the shapes of the clouds. As she lay there she dreamed of a life elsewhere, far from the cares of her own. It was hard for her to accept the way things were.

She was a delicate creature really, despite her physical features – a brawny frame, thick neck and large head covered in a mass of unruly curls. But her face was something to behold – porcelain skin and clear blue eyes. The kind that teared easily yet spoke volumes. Although her hands were large, as large as shovels, they were nimble and gentle, giving an indication of the lassie's tender heart. Her mother would refer to her as the cart, 'heavy and clumsy' she would laugh. There was a harshness, something mean in the edge of her voice that inferred that it wasn't a case of gentle teasing. Something darker lurked. Perhaps that was why Jenny spent as many of her waking hours as she could away from the house and, if possible, people. Perhaps she felt safer within the surrounds of nature, and quite understandably too. It seemed that every move she made she was greeted with 'No you can't' or 'Fat, lazy good-for-nothing'.

She never openly voiced it at the time but it was evident that from the day she came into the house she got pushed aside. The much-longed for son, an heir to carry on the family line, had appeared at last. She was only seven at the time, not quite old enough to fully comprehend, but had a tentative awareness that a light for her had gone out. All efforts to be loved equally became futile and so she merely gave up and withdrew – waiting, down on the banks of the river beneath the trees, to grow up and for life to really begin.

She never held it against her brother, how could she? It wasn't his fault. He wasn't responsible for being overindulged. Jenny would listen in the morning. Her mother's footsteps crossing the landing to her brother's room. The creak of the door and her mother's soft voice, 'Don't get up, son, till I light the fire,' and after she had done so, she would wake him gently and encourage him to put his feet in the hearth to keep them warm. She would then serve him boiled egg and hot buttered toast while Jenny was left to shiver and made to eat cold, lumpy porridge with too much salt.

So when the dandelion down flounced on the water and she spied a movement, Jenny was at once alert – alert to something that darted beneath the water's silvery glare. It was deep in that part she knew; last summer she had slipped and almost drowned there. Closing her eyes, she remembered thrashing wildly; submerging into the depths of the cold water, a constricting blind terror as she tried to breathe, scream, breathe ... before everything went dark. How she got to the bank she would never know, but found herself lying cold and wet on the dry mud, midges dancing in the gloaming as she coughed up river dregs and spittle.

Watching the spot intensely for a while she hardly dared move, let alone breathe. Eventually she relaxed and convinced herself that it must have been a trick of the light or perhaps a shadow cast from the trees towering above. Idly, she picked up a few stones from around her and threw them in the water. Plop, plop. Watching the ripples was satisfying. As she continued to scatter small stones across the water a song, a haunting melody, came to mind and she started to sing, softly at first but soon the banks and the water carried the notes and played them back in an echo.

A heron hefted out of the water as something splashed nearby then the water eddied not ten yards from where she sat. From the corner of her eye Jenny saw something emerge out of the water, first a head tossing a great mane so that silver beads of water fell about it. Steam rose from its glossy skin.

Jenny turned her head to look at this creature full on – a magnificent white horse standing so near and so still. He looked at her with his great brown eyes framed by long lashes. Jenny was transfixed, so many thoughts going through her mind: Who does this horse belong to? How did he get so near without me realising? And why is he staring at me like that?

Finally the horse stepped closer and slowly lowered its head. Spellbound, Jenny reached up her hand and began to stroke the

horse's neck, 'You are so beautiful.' Then, to her utter dismay, she found she could not remove her hand.

'What is this, what kind of horse are you?'

'A magical horse, the type of horse to be feared and shunned – all in the faery world despise me. I am the creature associated with nightmares. I haunt the rivers and streams. They call me the water horse, the Kelpie of the Wading Burn, for this is the place where Kelpies throughout time have come down to join the North Esk River.'

'But I have never heard of you, and you don't appear to be that frightening. Well, I'm not feared of you.'

The Kelpie looked up and its brown eyes began to fill with tears. 'I'm so lonely; all I really want is a friend, some company. Someone to play with in the water.'

'I would love to play in the water but I'm afraid I can't swim.'

'I know …'

There was a sudden lull as Jenny looked directly at the Kelpie and the thought dawned on her.

'Was it you who saved me that time I slipped in the water?'

The Kelpie lowered his head down and made to bow, a flicker of a smile appearing on his rubbery whiskered muzzle.

'It was you, wasn't it!'

Jenny lunged forward and gave the Kelpie a huge hug, burying her face in his long dark mane and arched neck. The Kelpie whinnied softly, clearly delighted with the attention he was getting.

After a while Jenny made to release her arms, stopping suddenly.

'What's this?' Her fingers had found a barely perceptible silver chain that had been hung around the Kelpie's neck. She peered at it closely.

'It is no ordinary chain. It was forged back in the mists of time in a faery forge. Look closer and you will see the intricate designs on each link. Magical inscriptions.'

'What do they mean?'

'I forget now, it was such a long time ago,' said the Kelpie. Jenny bent her head to peer at the chain. She sucked in her breath.

'Oh, I've never seen anything so beautiful in all my days. That's almost as fine as a spider's web.' She made to tug it softly in order to see it more clearly in the light. Although her movement was gentle, the chain caught on the Kelpie's mane, snapped, and fell. She caught it momentarily in her hands. It seemed to take on a life of its own, searching for an opening from which to escape. She lunged again, making a valiant attempt to catch it but watched with horror as it slithered through her fingers and dropped into the water. It swam in eel-like movements, caught up in the current, rapidly disappearing into the shadows and rocks beyond.

Jenny let out a cry of horror and brought her hands up to her face. 'I'm so sorry!'

Everything went still and deadly quiet. The Kelpie's withers quivered as the breeze gently lifted his mane. He turned his head to look down into the water, then sideways back at Jenny. It looked like his lips were parting as if in a cheeky smile.

Just at that moment a shrill voice boomed out, 'Jenneeeeeeey!'

Startled, Jenny made to move, a look of dread on her face. 'I have to go now. Can we meet again?'

'Of course, I'll look for you.'

Jenny scrambled up the side of the banks and with a fleeting wave and backward glance disappeared. A raised and angry voice could be heard above the sound of the running water.

'Where have you been, you idle good for nothing?' followed by what sounded like the smart smack of a hand connecting with flesh, and a cry of pain.

Early the next morning Jenny was back on the banks. Her eyes were still swollen and red from crying. Once again the Kelpie appeared beside her without her noticing. His movements were swift and soundless. He stood a good seventeen hands, all muscle and sinew with a coat that shone like a nimbus.

'I'm glad you came back. Are you cross about your chain?'

'I'm not that fussed,' said the Kelpie, absentmindedly pawing at the ground. 'Now I'm no longer obliged to carry you off to my home beneath the water. Not that I would want to, it's in an awful mess.'

'Is that what you would have done? Carried me off?' Jenny stared directly at him.

'Potentially.'

'But why?'

'Kelpies have been spellbound for hundreds of years now – we're obliged to do that.'

'Obliged! Doesn't that bother you?'

'Sometimes.'

'So what kind of spell is it and who cast it?'

'Oh, the water sprites.'

'There are water sprites around here?' Jenny looked around her rather uneasily.

'There used to be, but not any more now, which is a relief. Awful crabbit wee creatures so they are. Anyway, now I'm free of any obligations to them or to you.'

Jenny looked at the Kelpie askance.

'How would you be obliged to me?'

'Simple. If you had taken the chain and kept it for yourself I would have belonged to you and had to do as you pleased.'

'Oh,' said Jenny. 'So, what happens to you now?'

'I'm not really sure but I think I'm tied to staying in the water. The river has my chain, so I suppose it's the river that owns me now.'

There was a long pause. Jenny sat and looked out across the water and spoke out loud, as if to no one.

'I suppose we're both tied yet in different ways. I would give anything to be independent, free to do as I please.' She looked up at the Kelpie. 'You are my only friend.'

The Kelpie did a little snort and trot on the spot with delight. 'Come, follow me, I'll show you how to cross the water and when the weather is brighter, I'll teach you how to swim.' He led her to where the sides of the riverbank were less steep but where the water looked deep and murky. With a lot of coaxing Jenny stepped into the chill water. The cold and the exhilaration made her cheeks flush. Leaning against his withers and gripping tightly to his mane, she took one tentative step after another until finally her foot reached the other side. They both whooped with joy and splashed the water. Startled birds lit out of the trees and up into the blue grey sky shrieking as they went.

'That was great,' said Jenny, an elated smile on her face.

'It'll soon come in very useful for you; make your fame and fortune.'

'How can that be?'

'Ah, did I not tell you that I also have the gift of prophecy?'

'No, away with you! So, how will crossing the water make my fame and fortune?'

The Kelpie leaned forward and part of his mane formed a fringe over his eyes.

'Not long from now there'll be a mill running up yonder,' he gestured with his head. 'People will travel from afar to visit this area and you will be the means to get them across the water. People will pay you for your services, and handsomely too.'

Now Jenny was the one who was clapping her hands with glee.

'Yes, I can almost hear it now. Folk will come from far and wide and they will hail you by calling, "Jenny lass, wade!"'

13

MARGARET HAWTHORN'S EARLY YEARS

Mornings and evenings they all sat in the small cottage kitchen eating brose by candlelight. The fire threw out little heat so they were always cold; mud-spattered feet, hands red with howkin tatties or pulling kale; but that's what farm work was like back then.

Maggie and her brother Tam, a twin, would watch their father, the head ploughman, with silent awe. Always up with the cockerel's first crow, moving in the semi-light, his great frame and broad shoulders throwing short shadows across the walls.

Maggie adored her father – they both did, could find no fault in him, yet at the same time they feared him. He was a quiet man, not easily understood. Kept himself to himself. He was slow and steady, like the huge dinner-plate-hooved beasts he worked. Maggie especially found any excuse to watch him work – the horses knew what he wanted. Surefooted in the harness, heads down, pulling hard at the plough as it carved its mark into the land.

They could always tell where he was, even with the high hedgerows – you only had to look up and see the flock of birds lifting and falling, following the plough, diving into the rich brown earth for treats. Maggie said that if she sat really still and quiet she

could hear the ruck and clack of stones against the coulter, the dull thud of hooves, the strain of the harness. But the best sound of all was the sound of her father's gentle encouragement, clicking his tongue like a broody hen and the low tones of 'Walk oan my lads, walk oan'. The harness brasses jangled in time with their steps. She could tell when they stretched their stride by the change in the clinking tempo.

Maggie envied her brother. Tradition dictated that he would go on to learn his father's trade, spend more time in his company, more than she could ever dream of. 'It's not fair,' she'd protest; she was the one that was more keen, more capable.

Tam wasn't interested in the horses, or labouring on the farm. He didn't have the right constitution for it; he was more fragile than her and had less stamina too. She could outrun, outfight and outwit him – not that anyone else could tell, for they were the spit image of each other, blue eyed, wild curly red hair, and pale, wiry frames. So much so that blue veins stood out on their pale skin like embroidery.

Maggie knew her twin as well as she knew herself. Said they thought the same things on virtually everything bar one. She was a horse woman through and through, and he was drawn to anything to do with water; fishing, guddling trout, watching otters, skimming stones. He had even shown a rare talent for fly fishing with his makeshift rod, made his father clap his great hands with pride. Sometimes Maggie would tease, saying that the Kelpie would get him if he didn't mind himself.

They were at an age where Maggie had not yet achieved womanhood. Her slight frame showed no sign of womanly curves and she took full advantage of it while she could – standing in for her brother when he had sneaked off and shirked his chores. There were times when they deliberately changed roles just to see if anyone would notice, and most of the time they never did. Sometimes they could be heard swapping stories of their exploits and roaring with laughter from behind the byre.

One spring, when the light was different, brighter, clearer, cleaner, a full moon slung big and low in an indigo sky. They spent ages after supper staring up at her and making wishes. In the early hours Maggie suddenly woke. She heard her father stirring from his cot, quietly putting on his clothes. There was a light tap on the door followed by whispering. The ploughman drew on his tackety-boots, pulled on his coat and left the warmth of the room, leaving a rush and pull of cold air as he closed the door to.

Outside, there were more low voices and boots softly treading into the distance. Maggie slipped out of bed and ran to the window only to find that whoever it was had already disappeared along with her father. Where? Why? The cold air wrapped itself around her and she shivered. For a moment she hesitated, perhaps considering whether to get back into bed, but now she was awake …

Maggie tiptoed out of the door, careful to drop the latch softly. Then she looked up at the big benevolent moon. She wasn't the type to be taken in by the stories about the man in the moon or that it was made of cream cheese or crowdie for that matter. But there were times she swore she saw the outline of a hare. After all old Jake, the grieve, had often said it was the place where all the mad hares went.

A light was coming from the byre. There was movement and strange sounds. Maggie ran noiselessly to a dark corner and looked on through a chink in the wall. Within, candles flickered, and in the background horses whinnied softly and scraped the ground with their hooves. But it wasn't the horses that drew her attention, no; her eyes took in a most peculiar sight.

Five strange hooded figures stood silently in a semi-circle facing someone seated on a chair before them. He was holding something aloft in his hand. It looked like a small cloven hoof. Perhaps it was a trick of the light, or maybe her imagination? She craned her neck to see who was sitting on the chair but all she could make out was a black cloak and heavily shadowed face.

Barely breathing, she watched him gesture; a considered, powerful movement with his hands. A young man, stripped to the waist and blindfolded, was made to step into the centre of the semi-circle. Then one of the hooded figures took him roughly by the shoulders and span him round several times before leaving him to stand alone before the seated one. He hung his head. His hands were tied behind his back and his legs visibly trembled.

Then, in that byre, at that particular moment, the seated figure began to chant. The cadence loud, low and steady. A strange guttural language – like words backwards. Everyone stood stock still, even the horses, as if they were all transfixed by the power of the words. Suddenly, it occurred to Maggie, that voice … no, it couldn't be, could it? The same tone as 'Walk oan my lads, walk oan'. She tried to press closer to get a better look, and in doing so dislodged a stone. It clattered to the floor, spinning on its axis. The chanting stopped.

Quickly she slipped away round the corner and hunkered down behind an old barrel, merging in with the darkness. She heard footsteps then saw the soft light of a lantern fill the space. A deep gruff voice barked sharply, 'Is there anybody there?' The owner of the voice lingered for a few moments, the lantern swinging with the wind.

Without warning, a barn owl flew out of a nearby byre, a mouse in its talons. Its huge wings swept noiselessly past. Then the light and the voice retreated, leaving only the darkness.

Maggie's breath was quick and shallow. She knew she had been witness to something that was not meant for her eyes and ears – dark arts indeed. Quietly she slipped back to the cottage, before anyone noticed her missing, before her father returned.

Some weeks later Maggie was busy in the barn while the visiting blacksmith worked in the stable next door shoeing horses. Several ploughmen gathered, having the craic. Without warning, a horse began lunging and kicking, its snorting signalling distress. The blacksmith tried soothing it, 'Wooa steady lad, steady,' but needed more assistance. Imperceptibly the mood in the stable changed very quickly. Curious, she drew close to the door and looked out. By the time she got there, the horse stood calm with two ploughmen at its side. The blacksmith, bent with the horse's fetlock in his hand, looked up at the ploughmen with a wry smile, drew his finger across his neck and said, 'Hide, heal, never reveal – The Horseman's Word.'

Maggie was witness to a secret and she was determined to find out more.

14

BONNY JEANNIE WATSON

Ah now, I mind there's been a great mony changes since the auld laird died. The young yin ye see was aye abroad, they say he was o'er heid an' ears in debt. At ony rate, he would never spend a penny on steadins nor land, so as the tacks ran oot, the farms were on the market and nae richt folk would offer for them. So that's the way ye see sae mony auld roofless wa's. The land was let in grass parks and the cotters hooses were used for cattle sheds.

Doon the brae there were twa canty hooses an' big gardens, ma faither an' mither in the yin, an' Davie Watson an' his dochter Jeannie lived in the ither. Jeannie was as braw a lass as ever stappit in black leather shoon, she was a wee thing petted, for she was the very licht o' her faither's e'e. Yet she wis as guid as she was bonny and mony a lad would hae walked oot wi her, but I never heard her name mentioned wi yin mair than anither. Ye see, ma mither had a big family and by this time some o' them were grown up and workin. Mony lads and lassies were gaithered at oor hoose at nicht. They were happy days. Burns writes aboot Hallowe'en but if you had been bidin' near us you would hae thocht we had Hallowe'en ilka week, onythin' an' a' thing for diversion – an' Jeannie Watson was aye the heid wan for that. But by an' by, she began no tae join us at nicht. She said her faither needed her mair. This wis as natural tho, an' though we missed her, we didnae tak it ill. But aye dark nicht when playin at 'Jack strike a licht' in the cauf's park, I ran roond by the loan and cam richt up against a couple standin at the beech tree at the corner. Somebody opened oor door at the time and the licht let me see wha they were: Jeannie Watson an' young Hamilton, the minister's auldest son wha wis comin out tae be a doctor.

Thinks I, *that's the way Jeannie'll no mak friends wi' us noo. We're nay guid enough for her noo* and I wis sair angry, for although I telt her a' my affairs, she had never mentioned Gordie Hamilton's name tae me. I said naethin tae onybody. But telt my mither. She telt me tae tak nae notice. Ah, often did we rue that some o' us hadna spoken, an' we aye thocht if we had broken the ice, the lassie wid hae opened her heart. But ye ken folk are a' wise ahint haund.

Well, aboot a month after I had seen her wi' her lad, we missed her aye day. But as she aften gaed tae the big hoose tae sew, we took nae notice. But when her fatiher cam hame his first road wis intae oor hoose spearin' for Jeannie. We telt him we thocht she wid be at the big hoose. My mither wanted him tae tak his supper wi' ma faither, but na, he couldnae rest, an' he said he would change his shoon and gang and meet her. But he wis nae sooner oot o' the door when he cam in again, fair daft like, greetin.

'Oh ma bairn, ma bairn, ma bonny Jeannie's left me. She's awa' an' a' her claes wi' her.'

My faither and mither did a' they could tae pacify him. Ma mither had tae tell him tae gang tae the manse and get the son's address. He could'nae tak in whit she was sayin' at first. Then he agreed tae gang and ma faither gaed wi' him. When the auld minister heard o' his son being blamed for gangin awa' wi' Jeannie, he wis as bad as Davie an' said he wid start oot for Edinburgh in the morning an' clear up a' thing if possible.

When they gaed tae the son's lodgins he telt them Jeannie had come, but only tae borrow a poond as she had either got her purse stolen or lost it. He offered tae get the landlady tae mak her some food, but she wouldnae bide as she said there wis a friend waitin for her.

Here the trail wis lost and though a search wis made oor Jeannie Watson wis never seen alive again. Puir Davie cam hame about a week after an' he wis that sair altered, we hardly kent him.

He couldnae settle tae onythin – but wis oot an' in, oot an' in, the hale day lang. He wis aye lookin up the road for Jeannie, and ilka nicht he kept a candle lichted at the hallan by the windae. And mony a time when my mother gaed tae mak his bed in the mornin', she foond it as she left it. It had never been layen on. Davie had been wanderin aboot a' nicht.

Aboot twelvemonth after Jeannie had disappeared, word wis broucht by carrier that there wis awfu' news frae Edinburgh. That there were doctors wha hired men tae kill folk for them tae operate on. They said that young Hamilton, the minister's son, wis yin o' the ringleaders and had ran off tae foreign parts. This wis awfu' news, but we thocht it wid turn oot better for the minister's sake, and so it did. The authorities didnae think that he had been connected with the doctors in gettin subjects but a diary he left ahint him explained aboot Jeannie.

He said she had come tae his lodgin's no tae borrow siller, but tae get him tae marry her as she couldnae hide her shame ony longer. He wis frichted his neebours wid see her, so sent her tae Burke's lodgins tae wait till night when his classes would be feenished. When he went there both Burke an' his landlady denied they had ever seen her.

He only got tae ken her fate when he saw her on the dissecting table an' wis o'er frichted tae say onythin lest her condition should be traced tae him. Whither this wis a' the truth or no, naebody could tell. Some folk said he wiled her tae Edinburgh and gotten Burke tae finish the job. Whichever way, poor Jeannie lost her life among them.

Many thanks to Midlothian Archives, Midlothian Libraries, Midlothian Local Studies Archives: The Black Collection (93) from which the nugget of this story was taken.

15

MOROCCO LAND

I first learned about this story through a mutual friend and colleague of mine, the fabulous storyteller Tim Porteus. One year Tim told one of the closing stories at the Scottish International Storytelling Festival and this was the subject of his story.

If you happen to travel to Edinburgh and find yourself on the Royal Mile, near the top of the Canongate, on the north side, look up and you will see a compelling wee statue of a Moor, complete with turban and necklace, seated high up on one of the buildings. This statue probably indicates the long-vanished premises of a dealer in Morocco leather or a tobacconist. It was moved there from an adjoining building when the one that is currently standing was being reconstructed. Nevertheless, a fanciful legend is attached to it.

Way back in the 1630s, Andrew Grey was a young man studying at the University of Edinburgh. Life was rough and bleak and Andrew was witness to turbulent times, particularly during the riots following the coronation of Charles I in 1633. The cause of the rioting was Charles I's religious leanings, and his attempt to force a new prayer book on the country. Scotland, in particular, took umbrage. The majority of the populace had its own particular take on religion and how it should be carried out and was quite unprepared to have a prayer book foisted on it by a king who

supported a High Anglican form of worship while simultaneously being married to a Catholic.

Ferocious rioting took place and during one of these riots the provost's house was set alight. Young Andrew Grey was one of the many who took to the streets to champion the cause and soon found himself in the thick of things. The torching of the provost's house proved to be his downfall and unfortunately Grey was caught by the authorities and made to stand trial. He was found guilty of rioting and further accused of being the ringleader, for which he received the death sentence. On the eve of his execution he broke out of the tollbooth after one of his friends drugged the guard. Escaping across the Nor Loch in a boat, he made his way to Leith and from there, fled the country by sea.

Fortune was not on his side as his travels led him to become a slave at the hands of pirates. He was then sold and ultimately ended up in the court of the Emperor of Morocco. Grey was canny as well as diligent and managed to work his way up through the ranks of the emperor's court, achieving both status and wealth. By the time he left Morocco he had managed to amass a fortune from trading on the Barbary Coast.

Over ten years later, in 1645, while the plague was raging in Edinburgh, a large vessel, an Algerian ship, arrived at Leith. A detachment of heavily armed men, led by a Moor, disembarked and made its way to the Netherbow Port and demanded admission. The men parleyed with the provost and baillies; they wanted a heavy tribute to spare the city.

The provost, Sir John Smith, was asked to hand over his son as a guarantee of good faith, but Smith only had a daughter and she was perilously ill from the plague. The Moor, as it turned out, was Grey, who had returned seeking revenge after being dealt with so shabbily during the riots.

Smith only had a daughter and she was perilously ill Upon discovering that the provost was in fact a distant relative, he changed his mind and took a different stance. He offered to cure the daughter, saying that if he failed he would spare the city.

Grey visited the Canongate tenement where the ailing daughter stayed and after administering a strange elixir, much to everyone's surprise, the daughter recovered. The couple fell in love and eventually married. They lived happily ever after in Morocco Close, where the Moor erected an effigy of his patron, the Emperor of Morocco, over the entrance. This came to be known to the locals as 'Morocco Land'.

16

THE SHOEMAKER AND THE BROONIES

There was once an old shoemaker. His wee shop was situated just a little way from John Knox's House on the High Street in Edinburgh. The shop was in a prime position, with its small windows displaying its wares to passers-by. Unfortunately, the shoemaker fell upon hard times and his fortune went from bad to worse. He became so poor that it got to the stage where he had hardly anything left to sell, just a wee scrap of leather to make one pair of shoes.

That night he carefully cut out the shoes, making sure to make the most of every wee scrap of leather he had. When finished, he set them out on the table ready to continue working on them in the morning. Then he locked the door, checked the windows and went upstairs to his bed to fall into a deep sleep. When he came down in the morning he was astonished to find a brand new pair of shoes made and finished to a very high standard sitting upon his table. He did not know what to make of it and stood for a while scratching his head. He called to his wife, they both marvelled at the beautiful craftsmanship.

Before long, a customer entered and tried the shoes on. He exclaimed that he had been searching high and low for such a pair of shoes and having tried them on was delighted to find that they were indeed very comfortable too. So pleased was he that he paid over the odds for them and praised the shoemaker for his skill. Now the shoemaker was in a position to be able to buy enough leather to make two more pairs of shoes. Carefully he cut them out that evening and left them on the table ready to begin working on them the next morning. Again, he locked the door, checked the windows and went upstairs to bed to fall into a deep sleep. In the morning when he went downstairs he was amazed to find not one, but two finished pairs of shoes.

No sooner had he put them in the window when another customer came along, and bought both pairs of shoes. Just like the previous sale, this customer was so delighted he paid over the odds. Now the shoemaker was able to buy enough leather for four more pairs of shoes.

Yet again he set to work, cutting out the leather, laving it on the table ready to work on the following morning. He locked the door, checked the windows and made his way upstairs to bed to fall into a deep sleep. In the morning, much to his delight, he found that the four pairs of shoes had been finished to a very high standard. And so it followed that the shoemaker saw a change in his fortune and began to make a good living – before long his shop and shoes became the talk of the city and many people came to purchase his famous wares. The shoemaker was becoming a wealthy man.

One night, not long before Christmas, when the shoemaker had finished cutting out the leather patterns for the shoes and was setting them out on the table, a thought occurred to him.

'My fortune has changed drastically for the better, and all for the kindness of a stranger that I have been unable to thank.'

So, having locked the door and checked the windows and climbed the stairs to bed, he said to his wife, 'Dear, I would really like to see if we can find out who it is that makes the wonderful shoes for us. How about we quietly wait and watch to see who it is that enters the shop?'

His wife was more than willing to find out and so they lit the candle and left it flickering in the shop. Then they hid in a dark corner of the room, sitting silent and still, and waited. On the stroke of midnight two wee brownies tiptoed out from a hole in the wainscot. They were small, shrivelled-looking creatures with long noses and unkempt wild hair. Quiet as mice they clambered up and seated themselves before the shoemaker's table. The shoemaker's wife stifled a gasp for she could see their little bodies shiver – they weren't wearing a stitch of clothing and their fingers, toes and noses were pinched and pink with cold. The shoemaker and his wife looked on. The broonies were diligent. They took up the pieces of shoe leather in their long delicate fingers and began to stitch and hammer.

They worked so rhythmically and quickly that the shoemaker and his wife could scarcely keep up. It took them next to no time.

When they were finished, they cleared up the mess and placed the finished shoes on the table, then scampered off back through the hole in the wainscot.

The shoemaker and his wife went to bed that night in wonder. In the morning his wife announced that she wanted to do something to show the little folk her gratitude for creating the change in their fortune. She decided she would make them some warm clothes and her husband should make them some comfortable shoes.

They set to work using the finest wool and the softest leather. Working all through the night, they bent their backs to the task until finally, with the first broken rays of morning light, they finished. That night, on Christmas Eve, having locked the doors and checked the windows, the shoemaker and his wife put out the wee clothes and shoes on the table for the broonies. Then, having lit the candle and left it flickering, they went and hid and waited in quiet but excited anticipation.

No sooner had the clock struck twelve when out from the wainscot came the two broonies. They scampered up to the table and stopped stock still, marvelling at the sight before them. Thrilled, they danced a wee jig on the spot and quickly put the clothes and shoes on. The expressions on their faces were a delight to behold. Then they sang:

How great,
How braw,
Nay mocket claes nae mair.
Gonnae no have tae dae,
Wi' messin' aboot wi' shoon.

They continued singing and dancing around the room in a wild and excited manner until finally they reached the wainscot and disappeared.

From that day onwards the wee broonies never came back to the shoemaker's shop. As for the shoemaker and his wife, they continued to prosper happily until the end of their days.

This is an adapted version of the Brothers Grimm's classic tale 'The Elves and the Shoemaker'.

17

THE LAIRD
O' COCKPEN

It was some 200 years ago that Lady Nairne penned the above poem, which in turn became a traditional song. Cockpen House, the mansion of the Laird of Cockpen, once stood on a romantic spot to the east, not far from Dalhousie Castle. The village of Cockpen itself is set in a beautiful rural area which is particularly picturesque along the banks of the Esk and can be found just to the south-east of Bonnyrigg where I live, which makes it easy for me to imagine the scenery in the following story.

> The laird o' Cockpen, he's proud an' he's great,
> His mind is ta'en up wi' the things o' the State;
> He wanted a wife, his braw house to keep,
> But favour wi' wooin' was fashious to seek.
>
> Down by the dyke-side a lady did dwell,
> At his table head he thocht she'd look well,
> M'Leish's ae dochter o' Clavers-ha' Lea,
> A penniless lass wi' a lang pedigree.

His wig was weel pouther'd and as gude as new,
His waistcoat was white, his coat it was blue;
He put on a ring, a sword, and cock'd hat,
And wha could refuse the laird wi' a' that?
He took the grey mare, and rade cannily,
And rapp'd at the yett o' Clavers-ha' Lea;
'Gae tell Mistress Jean to come speedily ben, –
She's wanted to speak to the laird o' Cockpen.'

Mistress Jean she was makin' the elderflower wine;
'An' what brings the laird at sic a like time?'
She put aff her apron, and on her silk goun,
Her mutch wi' red ribbons, and gaed awa' doun.

An' when she cam' ben, he bowed fu' low,
An' what was his errand he soon let her know;
Amazed was the laird when the lady said 'Na',
And wi' a laigh curtsie she turned awa'.

Dumfounder'd was he, nae sigh did he gie,
He mounted his mare – he rade cannily;
An' aften he thought, as he gaed through the glen,
She's daft to refuse the laird o' Cockpen.

Carolina Oliphant
(Lady Nairne, 1766–1845)

A long time ago, just outside the village of Cockpen, there lived
a Laird in his mansion house. He was a wealthy landowner with
plenty of land to his name and gold coins jingling in his deep
pockets. He was not what you would call a looker by any stretch
of the imagination. He was short and stout with fat greedy fingers

and bulging eyes, similar to those of a fish. He had a wide wily smile that matched his pompous attitude. His mother had always mollycoddled him and filled his head with outlandish notions of being handsome and intelligent. Sadly this was not the case, but the Laird fully believed what his mother had told him. He thought that his looks, coupled with his great intelligence and wealth would guarantee him a choice of the lassies when the time came.

He strutted and preened, spoke on and about subjects he didn't understand, offended and ignored, completely oblivious of the adverse impact he made on those around him. The years flew by unaccompanied by friends or sweethearts.

One morning, while gazing at himself in the bathroom mirror, he spotted a few grey hairs and the odd wrinkle or two. Only then it dawned on him he had reached middle age without a wife and family. 'This'll nae do,' he said to himself. 'It's aboot time a had a wife an' heir.'

He saddled up his grey mare and rode out across his lands and just as he was trotting down a leafy tree-lined lane with the warm sun shining on his back he spied a hardy young lass working away in a field. He rubbed his pudgy little hands together and a smile spread across his face as he muttered to himself, 'Oh aye, that's the lass fir me. She looks like a good worker which will save me having tae pay her wages too.'

The Laird was not fussed about having a woman with fancy airs and graces. No, he wanted someone 'functional and appreciative'. It was a foregone conclusion that she would become his wife, after all, 'She's poor an' humble. A'll be a great catch; she'll tak' ma offer straight awa' nay doot.'

He pulled up his grey mare and called over to her in the field, bidding her to come to his house. When she finally arrived, she seemed perplexed by his request, as if she was not quite sure what to make of it. It did, after all, seem very out of character for

a Laird. He was smiling rather too much and sweat had appeared on his forehead, causing him to mop it regularly with his foppish handkerchief, and he kept looking at her in an odd way, certainly not in keeping for a person of his station. He bid her to come into the drawing room and sat her down on the ornate and overly-stuffed sofa. When he had her full attention he started to speak.

'So, lass,' he said, smoothing his hands down his waistcoat, stopping momentarily to look at his fob watch, 'it has recently come to ma attention that a'll be needin' a wife ...' he stopped, hesitatingly.

'Eh! A wife?' said she.

'Aye, a wife tae provide me wi' an heir ye ken ... for the estate.'

'Oh,' she responded. There was no doubt in her mind that the Laird had been at the whiskey.

'Aye lass,' he said, fixing his glad eyes on her. 'A've decided that yer jist whit a'm lookin' for.'

Well, the lass, who was taking a sup of water at the time, choked and spluttered, her face had turned red, she had gagged and dribbled down her dress and on the carpet. The Laird didn't seem to notice.

'Well?' he said, sitting on the edge of his seat.

'Really?' she exclaimed rather brashly, as she struggled to keep her jaw from hanging open. 'Am no fir marrying onybody, especially yerself, thank ye verra much fir the offer an' ... dinnae think am no grateful but ... yer far too guid fer the likes o' me, a mere ferm lass!' She made to stand up, but the Laird insisted she remained seated.

'Ach naw, a've made ma mind up. Ye'll dae.'

'Weel naw, a've made ma ain mind up an' a'll bid ye guid day, Sir. A'll awa.'

His eyes boggled and his face turned puce. No one had ever talked back to him, let alone refused him. Leaning forward on the edge of his chair, he tried again.

'I'd buy you some sturdy boots and possibly a pair of fine leather gloves for when you're working in the fields.' He inclined his head and raised his eyebrows, looking from her face to her boots to her face. She clenched her jaw.

'How about I give you time off on Saturdays as well as Sundays?' he said more urgently.

She frowned and clenched her jaw so hard that the muscles in her cheek twitched.

'Very well, you drive a hard bargain. You'll get an allowance, say two and sixpence a week, now I can't say fairer than that.'

'But that's less than I get paid now,' she exploded, her hands now balled into fists on her hips.

'Come, come, my dear. You know I wouldn't be charging you rent would I?' This time he used his charm offensive with a rather coquettish smile.

Her eyes fixed on his yellowing teeth; the two front ones were particularly prominent, not unlike those found on rats, and she had come across many of them scampering across the fields and barns in her time.

The more he blethered and dabbed his brow, the more strongly she refused him. The more she declined the more the Laird wanted what he could not have.

'Ye'll dae as a please an that'll be an end tae it,' bellowed the Laird, pounding his fist on the table, maddened by the lass. Eventually she left without accepting the Laird's offer. Hell-bent on marrying this girl the Laird sent for her father, a tenant farmer on his land, thinking that perhaps he could get him to talk to his daughter round to changing her mind.

Several drams of whisky were raised and downed. A few pleasantries were exchanged before the Laird made his requirements known. He gave all kinds of promises to the farmer. 'If ye convince her tae change her mind, a'll see tae it that yer debts are wiped oot an' a'll e'en throw in some land, perhaps an acre or two o' yer ain choice. Tis a fair offer don't ye think?'

They shook on the deal and drank a few more drams to seal it.

The farmer tottered out of the door and turned once more to reassure the Laird in a slow but steady slur. 'A'll be sure an bring her roond and dinnae mind what she's said, she's a young lass an doesna' ken things, she's glaikit ye ken … a'll be seeing yous then,' and he stopped to raise an unsteady hand in a wave before giggling the words, 'son-in-law'.

Back at the farmer's house things did not go well. Despite her father's words – 'Ye'll be the mistress o' the big hoose and there's an end tae it' – the lass was not for changing her mind; she was disgusted at how 'blootered' he was with the drink and at the deal he had made. 'A'll no merry that arrogant, miserly crabbit auld deil. No for a' the gold in Wanlockheid an' that's final.'

Days passed and the uneasy farmer did not return to the Laird's house with the news he was expecting. Instead he stayed indoors listening to his daughter shouting in the kitchen and smashing the odd piece of china; he half expected the Laird to turn up and turn him out of his home too. He didn't know which way to turn. Meanwhile, the Laird impatiently paced the corridors, stamped up the stairs and snapped at his staff in a gruff, agitated manner. Finally the Laird decided to call on the farmer himself. The farmer meekly told him that 'She's having nane o' it.'

The Laird was raging: 'A dinnae care how ye dae it, just get it sorted man. A'll no be kept waiting a day langa fir ma bride.'

There was no alternative but for the poor farmer and the Laird to come up with a cunning plan. The wedding details were to be left to the Laird – the minister, guests, cake, wedding feast and gown – and the farmer would send his daughter on at the agreed time. He was under strict instructions not to mention the wedding that awaited her; merely that she was expected to carry out some work up at the big house.

'Ocht, she'll be fair awa' wi' the braw wedding goun,' said the Laird.

'Aye, an affeared o' the minister an' sae overawed by the weel daen guests that she'll readily gie her consent,' said the farmer.

'A can just see it noo. There's nae way a mere farm lass wad refuse sich an opportunity,' said the overconfident Laird. And so the wedding was arranged.

There was much excitement and activity among the staff making the mansion fit for the wedding to the 'mystery' bride. The Laird waited for all the guests to be assembled in the great hall, the wedding gown to be Laid out, the minister in his vestments settled in preparation for the ceremony. Once this was all in hand he sent for the stable lad, 'Awa' an go tae farmer McLeish's,' he ordered, 'and bring back what a'm promised. Mind an' be quick aboot it or a'll gie ye a richt sair heid.'

The young lad set off in a hurry, all the time thinking, 'A' wunner whit the promise maun be?' He ran so fast he was virtually slavering by the time he reached the farmer's door.

'The maister has sent me tae git whit ye promised him,' he wheezed.

'Ach aye, there's nay doubt aboot that,' said the farmer. 'She's awa' in that field o'er there; ye'd better fetch her.'

The lad ran off to the field only to find the daughter hoeing turnips.

'The Laird has sent me tae collect whit yer faither has promised him,' he said, panting heavily.

But she was canny and within a blink of an eye she had figured out what was afoot.

An enigmatic smile spread across her lips. She stopped to wipe her brow then lean on her hoe as she looked down the field. 'Weel, ye'd best tak her then. See that auld mare grazing at the bottom o' the field, it's her ye'll be efter.'

The lad ran down through the muddy field, jumped on the mare's back and rode back to the mansion house at full gallop. Once there he leapt off at the door, dashed inside and called up to the Laird.

'Sir, a've goat her, she's at the front door.'

'Weel done laddie,' called down the Laird. 'Noo, tak her up tae ma mither's auld chamber.'

'Bit! bit! Sir –' his voice rising with surprise.

'Never mind bit,' the Laird barked. 'Jist git oan wi' it. If ye ken wit's guid fer ye.'

One look at the Laird's red and angry face told the lad that there would be a right stooshie if he didn't get it sorted.

'The Laird's gone aff his heid,' he thought.

So off he went to find other labourers to help and they set to work. The poor frightened old mare showed the whites of her eyes and bared her teeth as some pushed her rump, others pulled her ears and tugged at her reins. She was heaved and shoved until finally they got her up the stairs and into the chamber. There she was left with her reins tied to a bedpost.

With that job done, the exhausted stable lad reported back to the Laird.

'That was a richt queer joab that,' he complained.

'Now,' said the Laird, 'send up the lassies fae the kitchen tae dress her in the wedding goun.'

Utterly scunnered, the stable lad stared.

'Go oan, git oan wi' it, dinnae jist stand there. An' mak' sure she's goat her veil and tiara oan. Awa ye go now.'

The lad ran down the stairs to the kitchen to spread the news.

'Yer no gonnae believe this. Yiv tae go upstairs an' find an auld mare in the mistress's chamber. The Laird wants ye tae dress her in the wedding claes. They're laid oan the bed.'

'Yer at it!. Awa' ye go an' bile yer heid.'

'Tis true. A'm no jesting. As daft as it sounds, the Laird wants to merry a mare.'

The kitchen staff were bent double roaring with laughter, tears streamed down their cheeks they laughed so much. Eventually they pulled themselves together, climbed the stairs and dressed the auld mare in a fashion fit for a horse getting wed. Once that was finished the lad went off to the Laird once more.

'Yiv done weel lad, noo, ma'sel an' the guests will be waiting in the drawing room. A want ye tae throw open the door an' announce the bride.'

There followed much rumbling and clattering as the old mare was coaxed and poked down the stairs. Finally she stood, stamping and snorting with frustration before the door in the hallway. Suddenly the door was thrown open and all the guests turned their heads to look back at the bride-to-be.

The old mare trotted in dressed as a bride; a dishevelled gown thrown over her hind quarters along with tiara affixed jauntily over one ear and mane and the veil draped over her head. Having spotted the crowd of shocked guests, she dropped a steaming dung heap on the floor then turned and galloped her way out of the house.

The minister's monocle fell to the floor; the Laird was utterly flummoxed, the guests whooped and roared with laughter that could be heard from a long way off.

Apparently, the Laird never tried to go courting again.

As for the lass, there are those that claim she is now married, whereas others state to the contrary. What is important is that she lives happily, true to herself with the ones she loves and doesn't opt for the empty trappings of a miserable life wedded to wealth and status.

I first heard a version of this tale from the wonderful storyteller Bea Ferguson, whose warmth and sense of fun shines through this story which originates from Finland as 'The Squire's Bride'. My version has been adapted to accommodate Lady Nairn's poem with a sense of Scots running through the tale.

18

ESCAPE TO SANCTUARY

Way back in the early 1320s, about the time when John II was abbot, Holyrood Church and its grounds were considered by citizens of Edinburgh as a place to go for sanctuary in order to escape arrest or harm. Such was its popularity that whole communities of people lived within the confines of the Holyrood grounds. Some of its community members were said to live there for years on end. Curiously, its dwellers could leave its confines on the pretext of 'attending church' on Sundays without any sanctions being applied.

The small party trotted in through the castle gates – it had been a long journey back from Calder Muir. The horses were weary and covered with sweat, and steam rose from their withers. The riders, although tired, were jubilant; they punched the air with their clenched fists as cheers and whistles sounded around the courtyard from garrison members. It was a hero's welcome.

Our governor Thomas Knyton, an imposing figure, swung deftly down off his horse, grinning from ear to ear. As his horse was led away he clasped the hands and slapped the backs of the men who had returned with the party, laughing a loud resounding laugh as he did so. One man, a Scotsman, Robert Prentergast, he embraced heartily and praised him highly indeed.

'You did well, Prentergast. That was some find you led us to. You shall be rewarded handsomely for this.'

Prentergast hadn't entirely fitted in with the garrison. Although a supporter of Balliol, known to everyone – even to us English – as 'the Scottish Pretender' on account of his failure to take and hold the Scottish throne, we still didn't trust him. You see, Prentergast was a Scotsman midst an English garrison full of Englishmen on Scottish turf – a traitor to his own kind. So when we saw Knyton commend him we were all a little taken aback. But credit where it's due, he did lead the sortie to find a healthy haul up near Calder Muir.

Later that night at dinner in the hall, I'm sure Prentergast expected to be eating with the nobles on the high table. But no, he had to take his place with the rest of us below the salt. You should have seen his face, a scowl that would have unnerved the hardest of men. He just sat, shoulders hunched, arms folded and refused to eat or speak to anyone. You could tell he was nursing his anger, feeding it with negative thoughts. Knyton could see this too, we all could, and in front of the whole hall, sarcastically asked what was ailing him. Of course, Prentergast knew that he knew but just couldn't help himself. His response was contemptuous, certainly not how you should speak to a noble.

Knyton was highly displeased; and we all know to keep our heads down when he's annoyed. So much so that he picked up the nearest weapon and walloped him hard across the head with it. Blood sprayed everywhere. I'd swear I saw Prentergast's eyes roll about in their sockets. He went very quiet after that, kept his eyes down.

I don't recall seeing him leave but seemingly he exited the garrison later that night. One of the guards said they saw him leaving, the side of his face looked like a swollen loaf of bread.

The next morning I was one of the party travelling with Knyton heading into the city. There were six of us altogether, Knyton out front on his grey horse, for he always liked to travel that way. He was a big man, broad of shoulder and a commanding swordsman – I wouldn't have liked to tackle him at any rate. Then, just as we had gone through the city gates, a figure shot out from Borthwick's Close. It all happened so quickly we didn't realise what was happening. I was one of the two horses bringing up the rear you see. All I saw was someone running out in front of Knyton's horse. He pulled it up sharp so we all tried to halt. I heard a shout and then I saw a flash of steel, a sword's blade glinting in the light. Knyton took a good length of the blade and as he bent over in pain, his attacker, Prentergast, pulled him off his horse and dashed him to the ground.

Our first reaction was to help the governor; a couple of us got off our horses and surrounded him. By this time Prentergast had leapt on his horse and was galloping his way down the High Street. People were screaming as he bore down on them at speed, the horse's hooves sending sparks flying off the cobbles with myself and Drew Townsend hard on his heels. He had the swiftest horse in the garrison to carry him so really there was no chance of catching up. He headed straight for Holyrood to seek sanctuary. Right enough, by the time we arrived, there he was, on his knees praying fervently in St Augustine's chapel. It was hard to stand and watch him there but under pain of excommunication we didn't dare violate sanctuary. A few minutes later Lionel Gibb and Eddie Robertson arrived to tell us that Knyton was dead and that we were to keep guard over Prentergast, make sure he didn't leave.

When we were relieved of our duties by a small squad of soldiers, we learned that they were to guard the chapel indefinitely, that hunger would force Prentergast to leave at some point.

Luck was smiling down on Prentergast, for the monks were loyal supporters of the Scottish Crown and managed to convey food to the fugitive without the guard noticing (though among the guardsmen I heard tell that they became engrossed in some

game and didn't keep a close eye on what was entering and leaving the chapel). Twelve days we sat there watching that chapel door, waiting for that murderer to burst out. Every time we got a look inside, there he was hanging about the altar of St Augustine as though his very life depended on it – and it did.

It was only on the thirteenth day that we couldn't see any sign of him in there. Eventually we got one of the monks to report back. He told us that it was empty. I'm so glad it wasn't on my watch when he disappeared; at least, I hope it wasn't. Seemingly Prentergast managed to escape dressed in a monk's cowl and gown.

Two weeks later word went round the garrison that he had joined up with Sir William Douglas, the Black Knight of Liddesdale whose forces lay out in the wastelands of Pentland Muir. Prentergast was raging and seeking to exact a fitting revenge.

Sadly, Prentergast got his wish. Some weeks later he led a band of Liddesdale's men into the city. He knew his way around, knew how to move about unseen. We were sitting ducks just waiting to be picked off. They attacked and left over four hundred of our men dying in the streets and later, the following year, the Black Knight took back the fortress. And in case you are wondering, we never did discover who gave Prentergast the monk's habit. The Lord certainly works in mysterious ways.

It's not a well-known fact that Holyrood had the power of sanctuary until after the Reformation, when the right of sanctuary for all crimes was abolished. However, its grounds continued to be a refuge for debtors. At one point there were approximately seven thousand debtors living on the grounds, going as far as building their own houses and often seen pottering about the confines of the park.
Daniel, William S., History of the Abbey and Palace of Holyrood (Duncan Anderson: Edinburgh 1852)

19

THE MAUTHE DOG OF ROSLIN

My great-aunt Sarah is an amazing character, full of mischief and stories. For her age she does incredibly well. Still in fine form, she walks everywhere, doesn't smoke, doesn't drink and lives alone and independently in her wee cottage near Roslin Glen.

On autumn days you can find her foraging amongst the hedgerows for rosehips or blackberries to make her jams and cordials or collecting sticks of firewood on the edge of the glen; such a resourceful woman. Born and bred in the area, Sarah knows the land and its secrets like the back of her hand, and her memories and tales stretch far back. She will be reaching her ninety-second birthday this July.

I recall one time not so long ago, when my brother Jake and I had gone for our tea, we asked her if she had heard of any sinister tales about the area. Jake told us about a headless character that carried an old lamp and walked along the River Esk. We all laughed as we wondered whether it was looking for its head or merely had a very small imperceptible one! We pressed Sarah for one of her stories. She looked reflective and poured herself another cup of tea, then, warming her hands on the cup and taking a long sip, she began in a low soft voice.

❖

'I remember the day that my father told us to stay clear of the glen and never to go alone. He emphasised that it was particularly treacherous on dark nights and especially when a storm was about. "There's dark things out in those woods; things that you wouldn't want to come across," were the words he used. I can still recall the look on his face, it took on a strange white sheen and his big broad hands gripped the sides of the table, making the veins stand out on his knuckles. We were all spellbound and our usual noise and banter was quelled to a hush. The only sound was the hiss and spit of the fire, its light throwing shadows and shapes across the room which added to the atmosphere. My mother made to hush him, "Eddie, no. You shouldnae be filling their heads with this." He rounded on her and thumped the table. "I'll decide what oor bairns need to know. It's no about making them feart, its aboot keeping them safe." He stood, towering above us, and looked each one of us in the eye. "There's a strange beast oot there. A've seen it and I swear on the book that it's pure evil."

'When he said it, there was no tell-tale twinkle in his eye, a hint that it was all a rouse, a myth to feed the children's imaginations. His look was that of serious caution and we all took heed.

'If pressed for more snippets of information about this beast he would turn his face away and merely say, "It's no for the likes o' bairn's ears ... ye'll come to ken o' it all in good time." Unfortunately my father died around about when I reached ten and our family had other more pressing concerns to be going on with.

'Occasionally there would be mention of this beast amongst the adults. It was always spoken of in hushed tones as if speaking of it too loudly would somehow summon it up, or so it seemed. It was even said that in certain stormy weathers it could be heard rampaging about, running through the woods in a wild frenzy, its deep guttural howls and endless baying echoing through Roslin Glen. Sightings were few, but the odd extraordinarily large paw print was noted here and there, along with an occasional dead animal; a sheep's carcass or that of a deer found rotting deep in the wooded area with its throat ripped out.

'I was never clear as to whether this thing was real or imaginary. Some said it was the atmosphere or the poor weather that brought it out, enabled it to cross over from another realm. But all were unified in stating that it was a vicious, hideous creature that took no prisoners, made no exceptions; everything and everyone was fair game.

'Ever since my father had told us of the beast I buried the idea of it deep within me. It haunted my childish dreams, fed my vivid imagination. Nearly all of my nightmares involved what I perceived to be the beast. There were some nights I woke myself up screaming. It would be the same dream over and over; I was being chased through the woods by a large black dog-like creature, snapping its jaws and baring its bloodied teeth, intent on savaging me. No matter how fast I ran, it was fleet of foot and ran faster, gaining on me with every bound. I could hear it getting closer and closer against the sound of the wind whistling through the trees, rustling the leaves, and the crunch and pound of my feet running through the wood. I could taste bile in my mouth as the fear gripped me. I was all so vivid and real.

'My mother was always the one to wake me out of it. I would wake to see her face leaning over me, her voice breaking into my dream. Holding me close as I cried in her arms, she soothed my fears, impressing upon me that it was a dream and reassuring me that the beast was just a story. But fears of the creature remained ever-present in the dim recesses of my mind.

'When I was about thirteen, I went with my two brothers to the Gala at Roslin. We spent the day enjoying the fun and processions. We had tuppence between us and spent most of the time arguing over what we would spend it on. If I recall that's when Jamie got his first kiss from Josie Lockhart, we ribbed him about it something awful. Must have been true love 'cause they were married some two years later.

'My best friend Jeanie Hunter had been chosen to be a flower girl, which was a source of great excitement and perhaps even a slight tinge of jealousy if I'm really honest. I had been involved in helping to decorate Jeanie's house especially for the event, just as we should – all those paperchains, we were at it for hours. Her dress was the prettiest I'd ever seen. Her mother was a miracle worker with the needle. I was so proud of Jeanie when I watched her take her place beside the May Queen, dressed in that white dress with a garland of flowers around her head. I honestly thought I would burst with excitement.

'By the time me and my brothers started to make tracks for home it was late, well past nine o'clock. There was no bus or cart to carry us, only our tired and sore feet. Home was some distance away and we had to walk through the glen. The light had begun to change from dusk to dark at just about the time when our route took us through the glen. The day had been hot, sunshine all the day through, and although there was still a sense of balminess, the air felt close and heavy. A distant roll of thunder rang out, at which point we all looked at each other in horror. Fear grew within me and I began to cry as the sky lit up with a bright white flash and lightening forked across the skyline. Rumbling thunder ranged closer some five seconds later. It seemed at that moment all background noise had been sucked into a vacuum.

Everything went silent; birds stopped singing, even the trees and their leaves made no sound, not even a soft rustle or the creak of a strained bough. A strange kind of darkness unfolded around us, just like the cloak of fear we wore about ourselves. I distinctly remember having this sense of deja vu, that I had been in this situation before. It was as though my body was tuning into something. It felt sickeningly familiar. This all seemed to happen in a split second.

'Then it came, through the trees from deep within the glen, amplified to a virtual roar of bloodcurdling baying. The thunder was now overhead, and as the storm let full vent, rain pelted down, bouncing off the leaves and branches, coursing down the tree trunks as we stumbled on, driven by fear. Midst the loud thunderclaps we could hear the muffled sounds of crashing and scurrying noises further off in the woodland. Then there was this baying, deep and guttural at first and ascending to a high keening pitch. The unearthly howls appeared to be getting closer, as did the rhythm of a large animal running – running towards us at great speed. Its cries urged us to pick up our feet and move faster than we had ever moved in our lives, homewards towards safety. My knees buckled at first, my worst nightmares realised. Fear paralysed every muscle I possessed. Had it not been for my brother Tam virtually dragging me by the collar of my dress and screaming "Sarah, move!" in my ear, I would have probably remained rooted to the spot. Goodness knows what would have happened to me then.

'It was in this desperate flight home that I caught a fleeting glimpse of the beast. What I saw I will never forget until my dying day. Red eyes like hot coals and a gaping mouth full of slavers and razor-sharp teeth. Every inch of it covered in dark, wiry hair. Muscles of steel and bigger than it had appeared in my mind's eye.

'That experience stayed with me for days after the event. I hardly slept and had difficulty keeping my hands steady. The sound of a dog's bark would set my heart off pounding deep within my chest and it was all I could do to stop trembling. Of course Mother told us all to "snap out of it" and not to talk about it for fear of frightening the young ones. My grandmother, who had come to live with us by then, said it was just our vivid imaginations working overtime from listening to unfounded local folktale nonsense. She set us to work with additional tasks in the house and garden because what we needed was "something to keep our obviously idle minds occupied".

'None of it made sense to me. I had so many questions – I knew there was talk of the beast, some kind of dog; it was one of those

subjects that was whispered about but never really talked about in the village. I know what I saw and yet I was still left questioning whether it really happened.

'So, being the pragmatic girl that I was, I took it upon myself to find out more information and I asked around the older folk. It was Tom, the old retired shepherd, that finally told me what I needed to hear. He said that the beast was referred to as the mauthe dog. That it was part of the local folklore and then he told me the origins of how it came about.

"It happened a long time ago way back in 1303. Roslin Glen was transformed from a place of beauty to the bloody scene of the first war of Scottish Independence. They called it the Battle of Roslin. It all came about because a certain Englishmen, John de Segrave, then governor of Scotland, fell in love with Scots' beauty Margaret Ramsey of Dalhousie. She, however, had fallen in love with the Lord of Rosslyn, Henry St Clair. De Seagrave was incensed and petitioned King Edward to invade Scotland.

"Thirty thousand Englishmen came across the border heading for Dalhousie Castle. At some point they were split up into three divisions and went in different directions, they thought it would give them an advantage against us. But we were canny, Red Comyn and Simon Frazer miraculously gathered a force of eight thousand and rode up from Biggar to take on the aggressors. They surprised the first lot on the embankments of the River Esk, it was early morning and they came across them still sleeping. Those that weren't killed fled into the glen and met their death falling over the steep sides. Although battle-weary, our men then went on to fight the ten thousand English at Dalhousie Castle and after that, up on to the high ground above the Esk Valley at Moutmarle.

"The odds against us were outrageous. You would have thought we wouldn't have stood a chance but the English didn't have the knowledge of the land like we did and that was the cause of their downfall.

"Today, there are several place names commemorating the battle. Think about it: Shinbanes field; shin bones, so many of them were found there. The same with Hewen field; for the many brave soldiers hewn to their death, and see Kilburn brook, they say it ran red with blood for three days following the fighting.

"So, it was during this battle that one of the English knights entered the fray mounted on an armoured courser with a large baying war hound at his side. A brutal fight against a Scottish knight followed, both were well versed in the use of arms; lances and swords clashed and sparred but in the end the Scottish knight had the upper hand and the Englishman was slain.

The moment he fell from his horse his hound took up the fight and attacked the Scottish knight with a terrifying ferocity. The knight wielded his sword and ran it through the great hound; still it railed, savage in its dying fight.

"Later, after the battle had finished, the Scottish knight returned to Roslin Castle. As he lay resting in his quarters the great hound he had executed on the battlefield turned up as an apparition in the guardroom. A great wave of fear and panic ran among the

troops – the hound's appearance was seen as a very bad omen. For
many nights after its first manifestation the dog returned, earning
itself the name of the mauthe dog.

I thought it a strange name to call a dog but having really looked
into it I found that the old French for the word 'mauthe' meant
malice or bad, so it seemed right for its time.

"Eventually the knight responsible for the dog's demise had to
take his turn to be on guard. He was terrified. Later that night,

when the darkness had closed around the castle walls, the knight awoke, sensing a strange presence in the room. Suddenly the knight gave rent a bloodcurdling scream that echoed through the halls and corridors of the castle. The other knights and soldiers were woken by the sound. Petrified, they listened to the knight's blood curdling screams carrying through the corridors as he fled through the castle and on up the castle steps. It was a good while after the cries had died away before they ventured out of their rooms to find the knight. When he was eventually found he was mute from fright. They put him to bed to rest but he was never to recover. He died three days later without uttering a single word

about what he had seen. Ever since then the dog has roamed the glen, especially on stormy days and nights."

'I couldn't thank that old shepherd, Tom, enough for telling me the story and came away feeling validated after what I had experienced way back when I was a young lass of thirteen. Those of you who are sceptical, it is up to you to prove otherwise and walk the glen on a dark night when a storm is raging.'

Another nugget of a story brought to my attention by Linda Early, artist extraordinaire.

20

THE GREY LADY OF NEWBATTLE ABBEY

The following tale relates to Newbattle Abbey, once a Cistercian monastery dating as far back at 1140. It subsequently became a stately home and was gifted to the nation by the 11th Marquis of Lothian in 1937. Going on to become the college we know it as today. Newbattle Abbey College holds a special place in my heart, as without it I never would have gone to university. It offered me, and countless others, the opportunity to transform my life and for that I am wholly indebted. What follows is a tale I heard while a student at the college.

Sir John Heron was a knight of the highest order; his reputation went before him as a formidable fighter as he had fought many a bloody battle against the English when called for. He owned a swathe of lands to the south-east of Edinburgh, in the Gilmerton district. There he resided with his two daughters, of whom he was very proud. They were quiet and obedient. His eldest, Margaret, was considered to be of a very pious nature, spending as often as she could in the chapel on her knees in prayer. Sir Heron had other plans, he wanted her off his hands and married to his brother's son. It was a business deal, a way of securing the family fortune, the marriage would make them heirs of large part of the estate and the future of the family would be assured. It had all been arranged.

Margaret travelled the three miles to Newbattle Abbey on a daily basis to pray in the chapel. During her visits she caught the eye of a monk. He was awed by her naivety and piousness but her striking beauty proved to be too much of a temptation for him. By and by he seduced her and a romance blossomed. At the same time another monk from the Abbey had succumbed to the temptations of the flesh and had fallen in love with a widow who owned a farm not far from Gilmerton. Soon the love struck couples began to meet regularly in secret at the farm known as The Grange.

Then one day word came to Sir Heron of an alarming nature. His right-hand man told him of the rumours that had been circulating – that his daughter Margaret had been having assignations with a certain monk from Newbattle Abbey. Sir John could hardly believe the news. So enraged was he that he punched the informant squarely on the jaw.

That night, after supper, he spoke to both his daughters and made them promise not to leave the house without his permission and to never visit The Grange where the alleged secret meetings had taken place. Upon retiring to bed, Sir Heron decided to look

in on each of his daughters, to check they were soundly asleep. When he looked into Margaret's room he was horrified to see that she was not there. A thorough search was made but she was nowhere to be found in either the house or the grounds.

A horse was missing from the stable. With no time to lose, Sir Heron saddled up his own steed and, taking two servants with him, set out in haste to The Grange.

He banged loudly on the door and commanded his daughter to come out. No one stirred, not a sound came from the house. Furious at his daughter's insubordination and ashamed of her misconduct, Sir Heron grabbed a torch from one of his servant's hands and set fire to the thatch. Stone-faced Sir Heron and his servants stood and watched as sparks jumped and flew. A high wind was blowing and fanned the flames – the fire took and the flames spread quickly. Pretty soon the house was engulfed with fire and its nine occupants, including Margaret and the two monks, perished.

Sir Heron paid dearly for this act of cruelty. The cold-blooded murder of the monks alone was considered an act of sacrilege. He was left no option but to flee the country lest he hang for his crime. His estate was forfeited to the king. Sir Walter Somerville, a friend of Sir Heron, worked hard in an attempt to redeem his actions with Newbattle's Abbot. Complaining bitterly about the monks immoral behaviour and contradictions they presented he reached a settlement that was agreed on the following terms:

> That Sir John should make over the merk of land of The Grange, where the mercer was committed, to, and in favour of the Abbey of Newbattle, claiming no right therein, neither in property or superiority … and, that the said Sir John should, bareheaded and barelegged, in sackcloth, crave absolution at the Bishop and Abbot's hand, and stand in the same manner at the principal door

of St Catherine's Chapel every Sabbath and holy for one year, and paying forty pennies at every time to the poor of the parish, and one hundred merks Scots to the monks of Newbattle to pray for the souls of those that died through his transgression.

To this day, sightings have been reported of the grey spectre of Lady Margaret Heron walking the grounds of Newbattle Abbey in search of her lover.

21

THE LAST HIGHWAYMAN OF DALKEITH

On Dalkeith's High Street you will find a building dating back to the early eighteenth century, known as the Tolbooth. It was once a thriving hub of activity relating to the borough's administration; a place for law and order featuring a prison in the west half, a courtroom on the east, and a dungeon known as the 'black hole' below ground.

If you stop just outside the Tolbooth and look down on the ground you will find a circle of coloured cobbles. These are all that remain to mark the spot where the gallows once stood for meting out the ultimate punishment – death by hanging. The last hanging to take place at this spot was in 1827. The following story tells how this came to be.

William Thomson was a formidable character. At the age of twenty-six he was at his physical peak: a tall, strapping man with a broad back, big hands and wide knuckles that he was not afraid to use. He was quick to anger. Most of his friends and associates were afraid to upset or challenge him because of his size and temper. In today's speak he would be thought of as a hard, bully of a man, not to be messed with.

Thomson was more brawn than brains; he made his living as a labourer, and supplemented this by other less-than-favourable means, often working with others to support his criminal activities.

Most times he colluded with his younger brother, James, and his nephew, John Frame. To a large extent they were his henchmen and together made for an intimidating trio.

Such was the case on one cold November afternoon in 1826. Thomson set off into Dalkeith and met with a few acquaintances at a well-known drinking den. He happened to mention to one of them that he had in mind dark deeds ahead, even asked this associate if he wanted to 'rumble a cove'(slang for 'rob a man'). The associate declined. Thomson was later seen leaving Dalkeith in the early evening with his brother and nephew, heading out towards Cousland – everyone knew it was with nefarious intent.

The three lay in wait for their victim. They didn't have to linger long for farmer George Gibson to come into sight. First they heard the steady plod of the horses' hooves, heading home after a hard day's work. The light was beginning to fade and George could feel the cold air wrapping itself around him. He kicked his horse on into a trot and just at the point where he was passing a small copse of trees near the foot of Langside Brae, the trio leapt out, grabbed the frightened horse's reins and pulled the startled rider down from his mount.

They viciously attacked George, leaving him bruised and battered and, having done so, relieved him of his silver pocket watch, small change and *Scotsman* newspaper. They scarpered off into the blackness of the night, leaving the poor farmer lying in a broken heap in the cold darkness.

Thomson and his cronies didn't figure on getting caught, they thought themselves untouchable. The law and its enforcers took a very dim view of likes of Thomson and within a very short space of time were apprehended. They were dragged off to Carlton Jail in Edinburgh, ready to stand trial at the High Court of Justice. Their case came to trial in January 1827, some two months after the crime had been committed. All three stood before the judge for attacking and assaulting farmer George Gibson. It was a serious offence (also known as highway robbery) that attracted harsh

penalties. The judge proclaimed the case, 'one of the most atrocious cases of robbery every brought before a court, or presented to a jury'. When the jury delivered their verdict they found all of them guilty but asked that the sentences for James Thomson and John Frame be commuted to custodial ones, having taken into account their young and impressionable age.

The judge left the courtroom to deliberate further. When he returned there was an ominous hush as he placed the black cap on his head, a sign he was about to pass the death sentence. Standing in the dock William Thomson held his head high in a gallus manner and said 'Thank you' sarcastically.

Thomson found himself in a damp, filthy, cold prison cell – a sobering contrast to his life before. He was frightened and at the same time angry – angry that his brother and nephew should live. The jail chaplain heard the whole gamut of his raging emotions. Thomson went from anger to bitterness and finally remorse and sorrow, saying that he thoroughly regretted the life he had led. 'If I had my life again it would not be spent as it had before.'

The day before he was due to meet his maker at the gallows Thomson was allowed visits from his wife, friends and family, particularly his brother James and nephew John Frame. The leave-taking was heart-rending and many tears were shed.

At seven o'clock on the morning of the execution Thomson was bundled into a hackney coach from Carlton Jail and, attended by the sheriff and several other officers, they set off in a long convoy of horses and carriages for his final journey to Dalkeith.

Crowds began to gather around the scaffold in expectation of the event, scheduled for twelve noon. From within Dalkeith Tollbooth, Thomson and the chaplain prayed and a psalm was sung. Throughout all of this he was remarkably resolute and composed. At five minutes to twelve his arms were pinioned and he was led out to the scaffold. Taking the steps purposefully, he stood silently before the crowd as a prayer and another psalm were sung. Then he spoke, bemoaning his fate and begging everyone not to follow his example: 'Take warning of my disgraceful and shameful end,' were the last words he uttered. Then the executioner fixed the rope and drew the cap over his head, making him ready for the fatal drop.

Half an hour later William Thomson's body was cut down from the gallows and given to his family. Often highwaymen were hanged at the scene of the crime and their bodies left there as a warning to other potential highwaymen.

That was the last public hanging to take place in Dalkeith, but capital punishment was to continue in Scotland until 1963, when the last judicial hanging took place in Aberdeen.

22

MURDER AT
THE NEUK

Once, a long time ago, just at the turn of the twentieth century, 1911 to be precise, there lived a wealthy couple, Charles and Clarissa Hutchison. Their house was quite a sizeable one for people of their standing and was situated just a little way outside a town called Dalkeith in Midlothian. Formidable wrought-iron gates swathed in green ivy stood at its entrance, fronting a long drive with leafy gardens front and rear.

The couple lived happily and were well loved and respected in their local community. They were invited to every significant community event and attended all the balls. Clarissa had a new dress for almost every occasion and always looked charming.

They longed for a child. Time passed and none came. They sought advice from doctors and specialists near and far. She took unctions and potions, performed strange exercises and practices. She even swam in the River Esk in the depths of winter, but still to no avail. Then, the much-longed-for miracle happened. A son was born and there was much rejoicing in the household they called The Neuk.

The child was named John after his paternal grandfather. His parents simply loved and adored him, cosseted him in many ways.

He had the best that money could buy and was never refused anything. Although appealing to the eye, the child was apt to fits of rage and had a fractious temperament. He went through nursemaid after nursemaid with the change of the seasons. He would taunt and cajole them, pull their hair and call them nasty names, and he would always, always make outlandish demands. He was, to put it bluntly, a brat! His howls and screams could be heard from the nursery at the top of the house. 'Noooooooooooo! I waaaannnnt it NOW!' As the child grew he got no better. But his parents still loved him and wouldn't have a bad word said against him.

Then the day came when Charles and Clarissa decided to throw a lavish dinner party to celebrate their silver wedding anniversary. Sixteen guests were invited, eight men and eight women, upstanding members of the community and loyal friends all. The dining table was elegantly decorated and groaning with sumptuous food, the wine glasses constantly topped up with wine. Amidst polite chatter, cutlery clattered and chinked on delicate porcelain plates piled with exquisitely cooked meats and sauces. No expense had been spared.

The toast master, Alfred Corrie, stood and raised his glass, paying tribute to the esteemed hosts and thanking all the guests. Then he made a surprise toast: 'To the health and happiness of his daughter and future son-in-law, John Hutchison.' Everyone round the table hushed, some gaped in astonishment. The candles in the candelabras flickered as if a cold draft had suddenly entered the room. Charles was the first to break the awkward silence, erupting into rapturous applause. Then the rest of the party followed suit. Clarissa was so ecstatic that she almost swooned. A maid was called upon to fetch the smelling salts; always useful for occasions such as this. John himself stood up and made a curt bow and a short speech, something along the lines of how he couldn't wait to marry

the love of his life. No one seemed to notice that he had his fingers
crossed behind his back, especially his intended.

John had a vile and black heart. He had a flagrant disregard
for everyone he met. He feigned interest only when there was

something in it for him. Perhaps that accounted for the constant snarl he had upon his lips that was partially hidden by a waxed moustache. He was tall and dark but not necessarily handsome; his eyes were too close together – another indication of a fickle character. Despite having a fiancée, John was often seen stepping out with a different girl, in fact several different girls, from the most unsavoury of establishments. He may have given the impression of being a gentleman but this was a long way from the truth. John's lifestyle far exceeded his means and he was not above borrowing. He spent an inordinate amount of time 'trying his luck on the horses'. Debts began to mount at an alarming rate. He had even borrowed money from his future father-in-law, claiming that the money would be used as a deposit for a new house … or was that horse?

The dinner party was coming to an end. All the courses of food had been served and thoroughly consumed. The genteel womenfolk had retired to the drawing room to take sherry and coffee while the men remained seated at the table to smoke cigars, drink coffee and talk about things that refined ladies should never hear.

John had made an effort to be helpful, had even given a hand in making the coffee; he had very particular tastes. He wore an exaggerated smile as his beguiled mother told her guests, 'You see, my son is so kind and thoughtful.'

Then, one by one, not long after the coffee had been consumed, the guests began to fall ill, so much so they began dropping like flies. Pandemonium ensued and a doctor was called for. He arrived with his black bag at the ready and immediately began tending the sick, but such was the need for medical attention another doctor was sent for. It soon became apparent that a poisoning of some sort had taken place, but how had it been administered and what had been used?

During the night the situation got worse. Charles Hutchison and another guest, a relative, died, at which point the police were called to the scene. They were now investigating a double murder and the services of a poisons specialist were called upon. He had to find the cause and type of poison, and quickly, as there were still twelve guests perilously ill.

The outside world looked on with bated breath; news of the tragic incident had spread throughout the kingdom. Finally the answers came. Arsenic, the poison of the kings, had been used. But by whom, and why?

Dropping a small suitcase into the boot, John Hutchison climbed into his expensive red sports car and left town, heading south at high speed. Meanwhile, across town in Dalkeith, police were questioning a certain local chemist for whom, it was claimed, John Hutchison was working. The logs showed that a bottle of arsenic had recently been recorded as missing. Hutchison was now firmly in the frame, his father barely cold in his grave and his grieving mother too distressed to comprehend what was going on as their son crossed the border into England.

Immediately the police issued a warrant for his arrest and released photos of Hutchison to the national press. Wanted posters were distributed throughout the United Kingdom. Have you seen this man?

The whole country held its breath and everyone, or so it seemed, appeared to be looking out for the callous villain. Sightings of him were reported at regular intervals until finally he was traced to a hotel in the Strand, London. Teams of detectives were sent in only to find that the elusive Hutchison had left the day before.

Detective Inspector John Laing, a local policeman from Dalkeith, was sent out after him. He was a quiet man, short in stature but big on determination. Although he had had little success with his other cases (sometimes he did get things wrong), he was given permission to go after Hutchison and 'make haste about it'. It was felt that it would serve to 'give the man something to do'. When news came in of a sighting in Guernsey Detective Inspector Laing left in pursuit without a moments hesitation. Just seventeen days after the cruel double murder, the noose, as far as Detective Inspector Laing was concerned, was closing in.

Once in Guernsey, Detective Inspector Laing began searching in earnest. Fate was smiling down on him. Knocking at the second lodging house its anxious landlady confirmed that Hutchison was indeed staying there, she recognised him from his picture in the paper, and he was still in. She led the way to his room.

Cornered and caught, the weasely Hutchison initially tried to deny his guilt. Undeterred, Detective Inspector Laing clenched his teeth and spoke in harsh tones; he was not going to be confounded by this feckless character. Only when confronted with photographic evidence of his deeds did Hutchison finally crack. He admitted all and agreed to go quietly. 'There'll be no need for handcuffs, I give you my word as a gentleman,' said Hutchison.

Meekly he hung his head and followed Detective Inspector Laing to the front door but just as it was opened, he bolted and ran back to his room. The detective caught up just in time to witness him swallow the contents of a small glass phial. With a smug smile on his face Hutchison dropped down dead to the floor. He had downed a poison, prussic acid, enough to kill at least twenty people.

This story doesn't have a fairy-tale ending; there is no happily ever after. The poisoner was dead but was never made to account for his actions. His death was quick and painless, unlike that of his victims, but was it justice? Many didn't seem to think so.

This is a well-known local story told on the lips of many a Dalkeith inhabitant. The story is kept alive by Dalkeith Museum, who have recently taken to doing story-walks around the area and have included this one with all its Agatha Christie-esque detail.

23

THE FAIRY BOY OF LEITH

Sounds from the King's Cavern

I am their brusher and beater
I brush the beater for January
Their harps are the birch
I drum the corners, four points
North, South, East and West
I cross the seas to Kings who know best
I cross the skies o'er Kings who know less
I triple paradiddle
I drag up the gates
I roll down the hill
I drag up the gates
I roll down the hill
And when all is still, I slide home.

(Claire Druett,
storyteller and poet, 2012)

This is ma story, o' how it came tae be. I dinnae expect ye tae
believe it a', but I assure ye it is all true from where a'm standin'.

I wis born and bred in Leith, Edinburgh, in the year o' Our Lord 1660. Back then it wis a bustling seaport wi' all manner o' life in an' aboot the docks. I grew up in the squalor o' the tenements. Ma family, like ithers aroond us, lived a hand-tae-mooth existence, particularly so eifter ma faither died. I wis eight year old.

Mither sent me oot early that mornin' tae get some messages. She needed milk fer the bairn, my youngest brither, only six month old an' sick wi' the colic. Rain wis pelting doon as the carriages barrelled past. I loved watchin' the posh folk sittin' in them all poker-faced and la-de-da lookin' doon on us 'street urchins'. I used tae wonder whit it would be like tae hae a belly full o' food an' a warm hoose tae bide in. If I'd had a magic wand I'd ha' wished fer a meat pie the size o' ma heid an' a gallon o' ale, but in they days ma wishes were simply that, wishes.

I tapped ma way tae the corner shop. Using two sturdy twigs I played the railings, thrummed at doors, pattered the windae panes, a rhythm wis in ma heid a' just could'nae shake. Life tae me was played oot in rhythmic patterns, even doon tae ma eyelid's soundless blink. It all stopped when a passin' coal cart hit a rut in the rood. It made quite a bang sending the horses aff in tae a panic. The cart-man had trouble reining them in, they jerked in their harness this way an' that, scattering bits o' coal across the street. Barely had it hit the floor when all us street bairns went runnin', scrabblin' aboot the cart wheels an' horses hooves, pouncin' on every piece we found. Any lump o' coal wis a welcome treat for the range.

Me an' Frankie O'Dowd spied the same piece, it seemed massive. We both made a dive for it, all elbows and knees. I got there first, but he, bein' bigger than me, prised it oot o' ma fingers. I looked him in the e'e, clenched ma jaw and gritted ma teeth but he wasn'ae gang tae gie it up that easily an' peeled ma fingers back yin by yin. So I bled his neb. We ended up rolling aboot in the gutter, joined by the ither bairns lookin' on, jeerin an' shouting. By then we had lost sicht o' the coal, too intent on blacking each other's een. Mr Muir the shopkeeper grabbed us both by the scruff o' oor necks an' threatened tae knock some sense in tae the pair o' us. I remember yellin' doon the street, 'I'll see yoos later Frankie O'Dowd,' as I watched him disappear doon Junction Street. Only then did I taste blood on my swollen lip.

Ma grazed fingers throbbed wi' pain an' cold. But that didn'ae stop me tapping oot a rhythm. This wis ma favourite thing tae dae, tappin', drummin', thrummin'. If I didn'ae have ony sticks I would use ma fingers. Sometimes I amazed mysel', it's as if ma honds an' fingers had a life o' their ain. Gangin sae fast, a flurry o' activity an' sound.

The main thing I remember aboot that day wis the sound o' drummin' wellin' up frae a distance. It wis faint at first, but got louder and louder. We all ran tae where the sound wis coming from, Frankie O'Dowd too.

That mornin' ma world completely changed. It wis the first time I had ever witnessed a parade like that. It wis braw. The soldiers, all dressed up in their smart uniforms, three abreast marchin' frae a troop ship headin' up the street towards the castle in time tae the pipe and drums. I was transfixed. The sheer beauty o' the drum roll, the snap o' the drumsticks an' the booming big bass drum as the crowd whooped and hollered.

The drummer threw his sticks high in tae the air, let them twirl, then caught them like he wasn'ae even tryin and withoot stopping. He didn'ae miss a step or blink an e'e. It wis then I knew that that wis what I wanted tae dae. Drum withoot missin' a step as though it wis part o' ma being, like breathin' or walkin'. No fae me workin' at the docks as stevedore, coming hame late an' tired, hands blistered an' back bent double wi' pain. I had nae idea how I wis tae mak this dream a reality either but I kenned deep doon that it wis part o' me.

Later that day, I wis up Carlton Hill, I'd been messin' aboot wi some o' the laddies at The Top o' The Walk. We'd been cheeky tae wan o' the stallholders, stolen a pie an' when chased, scattered like nine pins. I bolted up the steps leading tae Carlton Hill jist as the sun wis gangin' doon. I really should ha' been hame but I kenned that the stallholder wis probably still aboot, I didn'ae want a skelping so I decided tae wait a bit longer. I sat quietly fer a bit – soon ma fingers were dancin' awa', drumming oot a tune. It sounded great tae me in ma heid. Next thing I knew I wis staring at this wee man, nay taller than ma knee, all dressed in green standin' richt there afore me. He had come through a wee door cut intae the hillside. I'd never noticed it before an' even if you looked really hard it would be hard tae place. The door wis wooden, a nondescript type o' wood, the top o' it arched tae match the curve o' the hill. Fancy markings were carved deep in tae the wood, pretty patterns an' swirls all linked an' looping. No sooner had the evening licht struck the door when the markings appeared tae take on a life o' their ain an' began tae shimmer an' dance.

The wee man took aff his hat an' made a long low bow. His face wis awfae handsome, fine chiselled cheekbones an' arresting

emerald green een. I wis momentarily dumbstruck. In a melodious soft voice, he said he wis pleased tae meet me. Even kenned ma name. He enquired as tae whether I wis hungry an' if I would like tae join him an' his friends on the ither side o' the door. Normally I would ha' rin a mile, but strangely ma feet were rooted tae the spot. The door wis opened just a wee bit an' a bricht golden licht flickered frae the ither side. Inside there wis movement, lots o' movement, whirlin' and dancin', the wild an' fun kind. Even more compelling wis the beautiful music. A mix o' heavenly bells, pipes, whistles an' fiddles, all in perfect rhythm an' harmony. Mair excited than afraid, I followed him, bending ma heid an' stooping tae step through the magical door an in tae the licht an' a huge stuccoed room.

Noo I'm back there every Thursday evenin, rain o' shine. Mither has given up trying tae stop me. 'Come hame lad,' she would plead, 'I'm feart for ye'. At first she greeted an' wrung her honds. 'There's nay sich thing as fairies an' elves' son.' She changed her mind when I told her fortune; the wee folk had gi'en me the gift o' second sicht. I showed her trinkets gi'en tae me by the fairies, craftsmanship like nae ither an' marvellous tae behold. But best o' all, they schooled me in the art o' drummin'. It wis a dream come true. They said ma passion fer drummin' shone through, so they took me in tae their musical vaults, gave me a drum, showed me how tae play it wi' and from the hairt. I learned tae play, play onything I cared tae. Like the sound o' raindrops or a tricklin' stream, applause, a jig, a reel, a strathspey, even cart wheels traivellin' across a cobbled street. And in exchange for this gift, I wis tae play for them on Thursday nichts. A small price tae pay don't ye think?

They held wonderful parties. Tables loaded wi' all kinds o' sumptuous foods, the likes o' which I had ne'er seen or tasted before. Then there wis the wine, the sweetest ye could ever imagine, like nectar frae the gods an' ne'er ending jugs o' it. And always, they were the kindest and most beautiful beings I had e'er met. Sometimes we would travel tae France or even Holland for these parties an' be back afore sunrise. Ne'er a dull moment.

At hame, in the world ootside the hill, word got roond that I wis drummin' fer the wee folk. Naebody seemed to question it. Sometimes folk would pass by then stop an' point – 'Look, it's the fairy boy o' Leith.'

Yin day, a lady frae the lodging hoose jist a couple o' streets away frae me, asked me if I would come an' speak tae yin o' her lodgers, a Captain George Burton, he wis a merchant seaman. She said he wis impressed wi' ma drummin'.

I turned up the next day, jist eifter breakfast. I wis shown in tae the drawing room. Captain Burton wis there wi' some o' his cronies. They seemed friendly enough, asked lots o' questions aboot the wee folk, ma drummin', where I'd visited wi' them an'

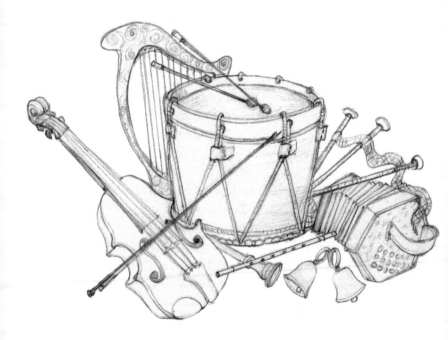

some o' the important sights there. Then they asked aboot ma family an' the school I attended. The captain seemed interested but no entirely convinced aboot the fairy folk, so I used the gift they gie'd me an' told him his fortune; tae prove the efficacy o' ma powers I told the captain that he had had twa wives, saw the forms o' them sitting on his shoulders. Both handsome women, wan o' the women asked me tae tell the captain that she had twa bairns oot o' wedlock afore she married him. It wis something that he already kenned but wis shocked wi' ma insight.

Time wis slipping by an' I needed tae be away, up the hill. The captain an' his acquaintances tried tae talk me in tae staying longer – I didn'ae want tae tarry an' found an excuse tae leave. They fetched me back again an' tried tae bar the door. It wis a futile attempt, naethin' would hold me back frae ma important assignation. The wee folk were no tae be kept waitin' – an' certainly no by me.

Mony years have passed since then. Three days in fairy land equate to seven years in oors. I hear tell I'm a legend noo, the Fairy Boy o' Leith. Ma story survived long aifter I left, for now I bide behind those beautifully carved doors, hidden tae all but the fairy folk, up on Carlton Hill an' I could'nae give twa figs whether ye believe me or no, fer now I march tae a different drum.

This is another well-kent Edinburgh tale. The first time I heard tell of it was from my very good friend Mary Bowron, who has now sadly passed. She was born and brought up in the Leith tenements and relished telling tales of Edinburgh's history and life.

24

THE SELKIE'S PLIGHT

It was a cold autumn evening in South Queensferry. Bitter, even, with the wind sweeping over the barren beach. Marion McRae sat in her cottage huddled close by the fire. Outside, the skies were folding silvery sheets of white to grey as though flattening out the last of the light. Greylag Geese took to the air and flew across the skyline calling noisily after the dimming rays and flying on into the night. With a resigned sigh Marion threw another clod of peat onto the fire then retrieved the warm bannocks, her movements slow and considered as she passed them to her seated visitor. They ate in silence. Carefully she brushed the crumbs from her long tweed skirt and spoke haltingly.

'It's been a long time.'

The visitor barely nodded. Marion touched her white hair, neatly plaited and pinned in great coils to each side of her head.

'The years have turned me grey and stiffened my bones – it's been a hard life, so it has. But you,' she looked at him full on, 'there's hardly a mark on you. Wider in the girth perhaps, maybe a bit slower …' she fell silent and for a while the only sound that filled the room was that of the fire and her visitor's deep rhythmic breaths.

'They cried that lass all the names under the sun they did. Never gave her a chance,' Marion fought to hold back a sob. 'Forgot all the kindnesses she had done for them … Aye, it suited them to think those things, made them feel just a little bit more special, self-righteous hypocrites.'

Her visitor inclined his head and turned to look at her, watching as she struggled to find the right words.

'She came to me, ye ken. Came and told me that she thought she might be with bairn. Looked at me with those big innocent eyes, all shining and full of trust. I remember the sheen of her long dark hair shining by the light of the fire. That and the fresh smell of the sea she brought with her. She reminded me of … she asked me to help her – to "Look at the runes, Marion, tell me what lies before me". Such delicate hands she had, pulling the shawl close round her tiny body. So young and vulnerable … I tried my best, but didn't see it for what it was …'

Marion remembered the voice of Betsy Flett singing in low ebbing tones and could still see her own buckled fidgeting fingers dowsing for answers.

'*In Noroway land, there lives a maid, hush baloo lilly, she would sing. Oh little ken I, my baby's father, nor the land that he dwells in.*'

'Aye, the runes' prophecy was no far wrong. The outcome was there, clear as day, but I didnae read them right. It was as if I wasnae supposed to know. When I mind it now, that was how it was meant to be.'

Yet Marion McRae had known, from years of being a howdie wife; having checked the soft swollen belly, listened to the rhythms of her pulse and smelled the sweetness of her breath that the lass was with child and well along too. Marion could not help her in the way she wanted. In desperation the lass had cried and wrung her hands, those delicate caring hands.

'My family wouldnae understand, they'll shun me; the community will cast me aside. I'll have nowhere to go. My bairn will need a hame.'

She pleaded and protested her innocence, hot tears streaked her face. Then she told her. The man responsible for her condition belonged to the sea.

'A Selkie? Are ye telling me that your bairn is of Selkie union?' Marion looked at Betsy directly and she cowered.

'Aye,' said Betsy, lowering her eyes and turning to gaze at the fire.

'We only met the once. Down on the seashore some four months back now – it was the night of Beltane, everyone was celebrating, I left early, my heart wasnae in it. How could it be? The men of my family were away fishing but hadn't come home when expected. We all feared the sea had taken them. I'd gone there to look for signs on the horizon, willing that boat to round the bay into the harbour. When I went there I swear mine were the only footprints on the shoreline. The sea was calm and quiet; there was still heat in the sand from the day. I remember taking my shoes off and pushing my toes deep into the heat and damp. I stood there watching, waiting for my eyes to adjust. As evening descended the light went from a soft yellow glow to a slow spreading blush. A whisper of a harr courted the waves, the mist and sparkle mingled like magic. Across the bay I heard the seals calling – so peaceful, so right against the backdrop of gentle sea sighs – shhhhh shhhhhh, like a softly sleeping bairn, all corried doon.

'Then he appeared, soundless across the sand. I got a sense of him standing barefoot next to me – wide feet, like paddles. We didnae speak, no for a long time. I kept looking ahead but snatched sly sidelong looks, his sturdy frame, the curl of his fingers and those whiskers ... finally he spoke, his voice deep and raspy.

'"They'll be back the morn. The north-easterly crosswinds held them back no doubt, but I'll wager they'll have themselves a fine catch."

'Although a stranger to me I assumed he was one of us, one of the seafaring community otherwise how did he ken about our boat? Before long we were sitting on the sand, just talking.' She had laughed with a warmth that made her eyes sparkle.

'When he smiled, my heart gave a leap. It was such a warm smile, one you could trust. I remember thinking that I felt as if I had kenned him forever.'

When Marion replied to Betsy she had spoken with a softness in her voice.

'They're Selkie people, hen, they're nothing to be feared of. Walked among us for hundreds of years now, mostly unnoticed. You should think yourself blessed to be visited by such a being.' Then she hesitated, her voice dropped to almost a whisper. 'Beware Betsy Flett, beware.' She pointed an arthritic finger at the lass and narrowed her eyes. 'Your child will be of two worlds and n'er the twain shall meet. You'll no need me to tell you to keep your counsel, folk round here will no understand and would want to do you and your bairn harm.'

A long silence followed, smoke belched from the fire then spiralled up into the blackness of the flue.

'There were nights when he came to me in my dreams. His voice, his breath upon me, I could taste the salt of his skin, his soft skin.' Betsy hugged her knees to her chest and began to rock back and forth. 'Sometimes I wonder if those visits were real. One time he came and asked me to leave with him, go and live in his world, but I said no. I was too feart. He pleaded with me, even telt me he knew what would happen in the future if I didnae follow – a harpoon would take him and our son.' She looked away, tears welling up in her eyes.

'The other day I found this shell threaded on a silver chain left on my pillow. In my dream he told me to give it to our son to wear so that he may know him. When I woke, I knew that was the last time I would ever see or hear from him. There has been nothing since, only silence to accompany the ache in my heart.'

Betsy began to sing a lullaby in quiet hushed tones:

'Awake awake, my pretty maid, Oh how softly you do sleep,
For here am I, your baby's father, sitting here at your bed feet.
I am a man upon the land, I am a Selkie on the sea,
and when I'm far and far from land, my home it is in Sule
     Skerrie.'

Many years followed. Betsy had her baby, a precious son. She cared for him and brought him up with pride, and was eventually reconciled within the seafaring community. She married a good man, a kind man, a crewman on a whaling ship, who brought her son up as his own. As the child came into manhood he spent

increasingly more time by the sea. At every possible opportunity
he went to the water, to watch it, swim in it, play in it. When
down on the seashore, listening to the tumble and roar of the
waves, watching them race and crash up the beach, he found peace
and contentment. His mother was too ashamed to tell him of his
beginnings so his affinity with the water felt surreal to him. Often
his mother chided him, 'Come away hame son,' she would say,
'this is where you belong, no the sea.' But deep down she knew
that the fear anchored in her heart would one day be realised.

Then early one May morning, the day of his nineteenth
birthday, his birth father, a Selkie, came to claim him, call him

back to his rightful place – the sea. The lad went willingly and without question. The only witness to this was the crewman, the man who had brought the boy up as his own, who held him in his arms, lulled him to sleep, taught him to ride a bike and fish. Yet all he saw swimming and frolicking in the waves was a great bull seal and its offspring.

The crewman lifted his harpoon and took aim. When he hauled the seals' bodies on to the boat, he found a silver chain with a small shell threaded through it around the neck of the pup.

Meanwhile, back in the cottage in South Queensferry, the fire hissed and crackled, throwing sparks into the night air. Both Marion and her night visitor sat in silence staring at the falling embers.

'Aye, if only I had known then,' she half whispered, half sobbed, 'maybe they could have been spared this fate and we wouldnae be sitting here now grieving the deaths of our son and our grandson. I should've been honest with Betsy, told her that I too had succumbed to a Selkie's charms, but fear and shame overwhelmed me and now … now it has come to this.'

A hand reached out for hers. It was soft and seal-like. The hand of a Selkie.

There are many Selkie stories to be found in Scotland – they are part of our cultural landscape. I crafted this story based on one of my favourite ballads, 'The Great Selkie of Sule Skerry'.

GLOSSARY

aboot	about	deil	devil
ahint haund	beforehand	dochter	daughter
auld	old	doon	down
aye	always	dour	stern
		dreich	bleak
baffies	slippers		
bairn	child	een	eyes
biding	staying		
bile	boil	faither	father
blootered	drunk	feart	afraid
bonny	pretty	frichted	frightened
brae	hill		
braw	good	gaithered	gathered
brither	brother	gallus	bold
brose	porridge	gi'en	given
broucht	brought	gie	give
buckie	a whelk used for	glaikit	stupid
	baiting	goun	gown
		grieve	farm bailiff
canty	cheerful	guid	good
claes	clothes		
crabbit	bad tempered	hallan	inner wall/
crowdie	a fresh cheese		partition
		harr	cold sea fog

heid	head	rammy	ruckus
honds	hands	richt	right
hoose	house		
		sair	sore
ither	other	scunnered	a feeling of
			disgust or
joab	job		loathing
ken	to know	shoon	shoes
kent	known	sicht	sight
		siller	silver
licht	light	skelping	hitting or
			striking
mair	more	sookin	sucking
messages	shopping	spaewife	fortune-teller
mither	mother	spearin	looking for
mony	many	stappit	stepped
mutch	hat	stooshie	a to-do
nae	no	tawse	whip
neebours	neighbours	thocht	thought
nicht	night	twa	two
o'er	over	wee	small
ony	any	wifey	married woman/
oot	out		older woman
		wunner	wonder
pouthered	powdered		
pratty	mischievous	yin	one